THE
IGNITED
ENTREPRENEUR

fuel for your flame

Sheli G. &
Terilee Harrison

Creative Force Press

Creative Force Press

The Ignited Entrepreneur
© 2015 by Sheli G and Terilee Harrison
www.sheliG.com | www.TerileeHarrison.com

This title is also available as an eBook. Visit
www.CreativeForcePress.com/titles for more information.

Published by Creative Force Press
4704 Pacific Ave, Suite C, Lacey, WA 98503
www.CreativeForcePress.com

ISBN: 978-1-939989-19-2

Printed in the United States of America

Endorsements

Wow! These two "ignited" women have knocked it out of the park with this book! From faith, belief and mindset to health, balance and superpowers, this book fuels the soul of the entrepreneur. Terilee and Sheli G provide the spark needed to inspire those who are called to create the life they want and deserve. A must read if you already are or are thinking of becoming an entrepreneur!

Kelli C. Holmes, Child of God, Wife, Mom, Entrepreneur, Founder & CEO TEAM Referral Network/TEAM Franchise Corp, **teamreferralnetwork.com**

Sheli G and Terilee are sharers of passion. Driven by desire. Committed to the challenge. Fiercely on fire. You will want to read *The Ignited Entrepreneur*!

Joni Pursell, Investment Advisor, Raymond James Financial Inc, Speaker, Humanitarian

The Ignited Entrepreneur is the most "meaty" book I've read when it comes to the wisdom of being a successful business owner. I've read hundreds of books on the subject, and this is the book that you will highlight, dog ear, and use in office meetings. Packed with guidance, tactics, and practical advice you can immediately implement no matter what industry you are in. Get it. Read it. Use it.

Mandy Keene, Co-Founder: Results In Coaching, **resultsincoaching.com**

The dynamic duo of Terilee and Sheli G help us to uncover and embrace our superpowers in this well written book. They do a fantastic job of covering all the bases and reminding us that mindset is the key to hitting personal home runs. I highly recommend this read for anyone wanting to take charge of their life and business.

Brett Labit, Founder, LIZ Global, Inc., **localimpactzone.com**

Sheli G and Terilee diligently demonstrate hard work, collaboration, and fierce conviction for our Creator that truly inspires people (including me) to stretch themselves and embrace their unique, beautiful paths in life. If you need something to light the fire within you, with this book, you have found your match. (All puns intended.)

Megan Bryant, Creator/Director, Idaho Laugh Fest, **idaholaughfest.com**

Dedication

The Ignited Entrepreneur is dedicated to the thousands of business owners we have had the honor and privilege of serving over the last ten years. You are inspiring. Knowing you has increased our learning. The relationships with each of you has made our lives richer. Because of our mutual experiences with you in business and in life, we are better people. We are grateful. You have all truly fueled the flame within us. It is our prayer and intention this book will return the favor and fuel the flame within you.

Acknowledgements – Sheli G

God:
Always the first to receive my gratitude is God. He downloaded in me my calling, career, and this book, too. He blesses me so often and much, I am just in gratitude constantly. Everything truly ignited and valuable in me, comes from Him.

My Family:
My soul-mate, Steve, who is adorable, witty, and allows me to be all of me (which is a handful), and our beautiful kids Tyger, Teisha, and Trae. They are such a huge blessing. They love me even when I'm writing a book at midnight. I can't wait to celebrate some of my recent crazy victories (including this book) with them on our family vacation.

My mom and dad, Ralph and Sherry Yerkes:
You taught me hard work, passion, loving God, laughter, giving, serving, writing, speaking, and singing. You've ignited the soul inside of me since birth. I am eternally humbled and honored to be your daughter and so very grateful.

Angie Shea, my sister:
My biggest fan. My life-long friend. And now, together, we are collaborating on some joint ignited ventures. I'm so blessed. Thank you, Angie, A.K.A. the Angel.

My Terilee:
My Co-Author, confidant and best friend, Terilee Harrison, has been my accountability buddy on this, my first book. (I've been trying to get a book done for ten years!) I just love you – mucho grande. You are an inspiration to me, a joy beam, freakin' hilarious, and an amazing Co-Facilitator in our transformational workshops too. #BOOM. I am always ignited by our collaboration and connection (and our laughter, especially when we both snort simultaneously).

Ray and Star, "Dad and Mom Gartman":
Steve's folks have always been loving, Godly, huge supporters of Steve and I and of my calling as well. I would NOT be where I am today without them, I am forever so grateful.

Other amaze-able souls who supported this journey:
Renee Settle for encouraging us and being on our team. Trevor Allen, another dear friend, who graced us with his art genius on the cover and the chapter icon images. You rock! Derrick Boles, another partner of mine in life and business, you came along at the right time to show me that there are authentic others who think GINORMOUSLY and are truly committed to changing the world. And, one of my many mentors that fueled my flame bigtime, Les Brown. You are a legit inspiration in every way possible. Being on your Speakers team for a time was an honor times a million. I am blessed by you all, and so many other mentors and friends who are not mentioned here. I love you.

Tyger:
I especially want to honor and dedicate this book to my son, Tyger. Although he is not my son by DNA, I married Steve who had Tyger (who was then four years old), and in my spirit, I adopted this young boy into my heart, forever. Today, Tyger is 17. He just finished up his time at a military school in Idaho that has challenged him on every level. He has courageously been rising up to it all and conquering like a Warrior-Boss. He has also started ideating about his first business. He is already fueling his own brilliant spark. That's my boy.

Acknowledgements – Terilee Harrison

God:
I am in absolute awe of the things God has done for me in my life. I pray I will use the talents He has given me throughout the rest of my life to show others how they can find Him.

Terry, Jackie, and Cole:
My family is one of my greatest gifts on this earth. You are each unique and extraordinary, and I love you with all my heart. Thank you for supporting me in my work.

My Parents, Jim and Bobbie Tussing:
Many people reading this book only wish they had the amazing, loving, and supportive parents I have been blessed with. Dad, I love you. Mom, I miss you every day, and I cannot wait to see you again.

Sheli G:
You inspire me. You help bring out the best in me. You make me laugh. I am beyond grateful for your friendship. God gave me a most amaze-able gift when He brought you into my life. Most of all, I love working with you and helping to bring people to a place of transformation and breakthrough. (P.S. It's not really work, is it?)

Amazing supporters of *The Ignited Entrepreneur:*
Renee Settle: Thank you for helping to draw out the best in my writing and encouraging me to tell my stories. Trevor Allen: You are an inspiration to me. Thank you for our amazing cover design and the chapter icons. Thank you for sharing your gifts and talents with us. I would adopt you if I could. Krista Dunk and Deborah McLain of Creative Force Press: Your professionalism, friendship, support, and expertise in bringing this book to print is *so* appreciated.

Contents

The Ignited Entrepreneur is Real. Really.

Foreword

Watching and observing people has been one of my gifts. Watching how people interact, how they share, how they dream, how they move, and how they grow is a very interesting process. Sheli G and Terilee Harrison have both expanded my faith and belief in how our actions can inspire, engage, and ignite others to greatness. From my observations over the last few years, I have seen the power of their faith and belief systems in action. The manifestation of this book you are about to read is a direct reflection of who they are as women, as leaders, and as world changers.

Most people operate in a space of fear and insecurity. Both Sheli and Terilee have become pacesetters in the personal development, human development, and spiritual development!

The Ignited Entrepreneur is the "what's next" in how business and life will operate in the near future. Both Terilee and Sheli G hit the nail on the head with their insights and practical, relevant stories. This book will help anyone (and everyone!) who is looking to improve their life experience. They have put together a systemic process that can help you examine and develop what is ready to be ignited within your soul. Enjoy!

Derrick Boles, Founder & CEO
STAND UP AMERICA
BOLES UNIVERSITY
www.derrickboles.com

Introduction

It starts with a **spark**.
A vision. A thought. An idea.
A Divine Download.
It takes one who is open, willing, and somehow searching. Searching for the call. The purpose. We all have one, after all. To do something significant. To help advance the world in some way…

From the micro to the macro, ideas that are birthed from human genius abound.
A new way of thinking.
A fresh approach to wellness.
A new solution for business.
A cause. A cure. A key…
Do you have it in you?

Are you open to the ideas, the possibilities...the scope of what could be?
Is your mind, and perhaps your heart, a fertile field for the seed of a dream to take hold and grow?
If not you, then who?
If not now, then when?
And, why not you, and now?! *Let's go.*

Many could, if only they stood still for a moment…
The moment that you ask yourself, "Am I open? Is it possible that I am capable of something so great, so much bigger than myself?"
Is your moment of reckoning, of awakening, of transformation at hand?

If you choose to walk in bravery, in the uncertain, in the juice of risk-taking, you're ready.
You may already be there.
You may be yet becoming.

Or, you may be just starting to explore even now…
The Ignited Entrepreneur in you.

Welcome to the community of those who fuel the fire in themselves and in others. ~ Sheli G

The Ignited Entrepreneur
Enrolls and Expands

If we are called to it — a career, a role, a business, or a cause — we enroll others into it through our words, in our deeds, and in our very energy. It's not easy, but it's necessary. We are all salespeople, because we are all enrolling someone into something all the time. We enroll others into what we believe in. What are you enrolling others into? ~ Sheli G

Chapter 1: Belief
by Terilee

When you truly believe in yourself, others won't be able to help but believe in you, too. ~ Terilee Harrison

If you're struggling to believe in yourself, surround yourself with some people who have massive belief in you. It will rub off. ~ Sheli G

From a friend of mine: "When I was seven years old, I believed I would be the first woman to walk on Mars. I dreamed of walking the catwalk to the open capsule that would take me there. I used to pretend my grandfather's old chaps were space pants and his leather welding jacket was my top. I made a cardboard and aluminum helmet, and with my cowboy boots, I was the perfect astronaut. I would bounce around the woodpile and out into the desert, pretending it was the Martian landscape. I honestly believed it would happen. I dreamed of the worlds I would explore."

"I believe in me."

When my son, Cole, was around five years old, he would often describe to me the amazing inventions he was going to create one day and about the super-humongous mansion he was going to live in. He always promised me there would be a spot for me on the 5th floor. He believed 100 percent in his ability to create and run a powerful company, and his success was guaranteed. Do you remember believing in yourself that much?

The Message

What is the difference between belief and faith? Belief means you acknowledge the truth of something. Faith means you trust it.

Think about it. What were you like as a child? You may or may not remember, but you were an amazing miracle!

You were curious. Creative. Innocent. Happy. Needy. Free. Funny. Stubborn. Brave. Loving. Smart. And, more!

Then, the world got in the way. It happens to all of us. From the same astronaut dreamer: "I think what made my belief change was when I told my third grade teacher and she said, 'Girls can't be astronauts. It's too dangerous.' I realized that my belief was wrong according to the authority in my life. It was devastating. I went home and cried for hours. When I was done, I got up, jaded, and went looking for a belief of what girls *could* do."

What are some ways the world affected you? Were you told "no"? Did you get in trouble? Did people hurt you physically or emotionally? Did Hollywood movies and television shows affect you? The media insinuates the message that you are not good enough and tells you through pictures and visual stories *you'll never amount to anything* or *this is all your fault.*

Being told "no" or being hurt changes you. It can change everything about you. It can be devastating the moment these untruths come crashing down upon your life. Your young soul is crushed when you take on the message that you are no longer free, confident, or worthy. *Losing belief in yourself is numbing.*

How does a negative mindset or low self-worth cause you to react? Your once-free soul tries desperately to protect itself, causing you to be guarded and defensive. You may seek to control matters in your life to avoid being hurt any more. You may feel conflict or feel fearful. Instead of knowing with your whole heart you can take on the world, you just might not try. You may stuff your past deep down inside, because it is just too painful to deal with. Your communication may get strained, or you may not say what's really on your mind. What's worse, you may self-sabotage to keep yourself from the success you no longer believe you deserve or self-medicate to cover up your intense pain.

Do you see yourself in this scenario? How have you changed?
This can be very painful to observe, but in order to believe in yourself again, it is imperative that you understand where you have been to continue on the road to where you are going. The good news is no matter what's happened to you or what you have done, you are still like a child. You are innocent, free, and brave. You are very powerful! *You know how powerful you are!*

Here is the good news! *Self-belief is learnable.*
It's never too late to cultivate self-belief. It may take some work, and it may require some getting real about your past, but it is absolutely possible to change from someone who doesn't like yourself to someone who believes in yourself.

Strengths
It's important to understand and embrace your strengths. Have you ever thought something like, "I can't be a nurse because I'm not good at math?" Being confident in what you are good at helps build confidence. *Building your strengths helps you shine even more in the world.*

Practice
The more experience you have, the more belief you will have that you *can* accomplish something. For example, let's say public

15

speaking. Public speaking is a huge fear for many people. Have you ever gotten butterflies, sweaty palms, or felt your entire body shake when it was your turn to speak somewhere? I know it used to happen to me, but the more you do it, the more calm you will feel. Over time, you will know, "I've got this. I can do this!" Practice and gaining experience is a key to self-belief and success.

What you believe about yourself on the inside is what you will manifest on the outside.
When you believe you can accomplish something, you will. When you have any doubt, I bet you will quit (or find some excuse).

If you know anything at this moment, know that I believe in you!

Fuel for your flame:
On an honest scale of 1 to 10, how much do you believe in yourself? Why did you give yourself that rating?
What, specifically, do you believe you can bring or accomplish? Put it in writing.

Chapter 2: Superpowers
by Sheli G

You have brilliance in you. Everyone does. You have something that only YOU can do, in the way that you can do it, once your giftings are maximized. ~ Sheli G

We have God-given strengths. I like to call these strengths our *Superpowers*, which sounds sexy and cool, don't you think?

The Message

I have come to think of our gifts as our superpowers. Right now, our culture is really into Marvel comic book heroes.

One of my personal faves is Iron Man. Not only is Tony Stark hot, but I love the pithy, funny writing that matches his quick wit. His suit is, of course, fabulous! I just realized I probably love the fact that his character is a crazy, visionary entrepreneur and a bit of a rule breaker! Okay, I digress...but I think we *all* have superpowers, too. I don't think we're gods, but I *do* believe that every person is not only born with a purpose, but also with innate strengths, gifts, talents, abilities, or whatever you choose to call them. And, these strengths enable us to fulfill that calling and be inspired long-term by it, too.

These innate gifts that we are honored with at birth deserve to be cultivated, nurtured, and strengthened. This creates the platform for us to use these gifts to their highest and best levels of effectiveness. It takes time – it's a process. It also takes life experience, a ton of patience, education, practice, mentoring, feedback from others, and so on.

These fine-tuning modalities help us not only to understand what our gifts are, but also what our strengths *are not*. I coach people, both professionally and personally, and this often comes up.

There are a ton of things that we *can* do.
We can make it work. We can learn skills or trades in hundreds of areas, industries, or positions. That doesn't mean it's your highest and best strength or that you will like it, *especially long term*. And, it doesn't mean that someone else can't knock it out of the park better than you! Let's be honest, we *want* to rock our position, role, business, or cause. *We want to be the best or the top percentile in our results, and have the joy that comes from living in our giftings.*

If you think you're the best at everything or even most things, you probably deserve to increase your awareness by taking the StrengthsFinders© test by Gallup, and get some professional coaching (without the coaching it's pretty pointless, by the way).

No one is good at everything – not at the high success levels we are talking about. Remember when you've seen someone in a role and you were thinking, "Woah, they are phenomenal! They are an incredible teacher, speaker, writer, coach, singer, leader, artist, cool mom, or CEO," etc.? People often describe them as "a natural" or "born with it." To the degree that you get goose-bumps, or learn at a profound level, or you see them move virtual mountains with their giftings, they are most likely living in their superpowers. They seem to have a supernatural skill that rises above the noise of their competition and everyone else around them. They almost make it look easy. Also, they usually seem pretty fired up to be doing what they are doing. They have a grounded confidence (hopefully not ego-driven cockiness… yawn). They are not smarter than you, more gifted than you, or superior to you. *They are in their sweet zone that breeds consistent, sustainable success.*

The good news is: *You* can experience your sweet zone, too!
We all have these gifts when we are born, but we aren't aware of them yet. And, we certainly don't know how to access them, harness them, and use them to their highest ability for the greater good. *This all has to be learned.*

I liken this to the pilot who finds him/herself in a beautiful, billion dollar F-18 super fighter plane. That is like us at birth! We are born with a brain, body, and incredible abilities, although we have no idea what we have, much less how to use it! Then, we learn just a few of the controls in the "cockpit" of us. We start walking, talking, and we begin to see some of our gifts come out. But, they are raw, immature, underdeveloped, awkward, and uneducated. They are lacking in experience, schooling, maturity, and life. So, the three controls in our amazing plane's cockpit (that we begin to discover as toddlers) can make flying that ga-zillion dollar, beautiful plane *scary at best*.

At first we are clumsy, inappropriate, rude at times, and over-confident as we start to learn...because we don't yet know what we don't know!
If we're not careful, or if we're without the blessing of good parenting and wise mentoring around us, we crash. We burn up. We possibly even burnout. We unintentionally (but successfully) acquire a lot of damage to our beautiful plane, inside and out, as we attempt to navigate this vehicle we were born into. *Can you relate to this?*

No matter what your upbringing was like or what your access to mentors has been, as adults, we are always at choice. We can wake up, become aware of our needs, and facilitate intentional self-growth in cultivating these superpowers, even if we feel like we are getting started later than some.

The critical thing is: *start now or continue from wherever you are.*
When you *do* become aware, activate. Mobilize yourself to become educated however that journey might look for you. Mastermind and brainstorm with others who you trust and respect, so you get objective perspectives and unleash your superpowers like Iron Man! It's never too late, unless you are not breathing anymore. True statement. And, if you're reading this, you're breathing! That's good news! You have brilliance in you. Everyone does. *You have something that only you can do, in the way*

that only you can, once your giftings are realized and totally maximized.

It takes feedback from other people to help us understand what our strengths are and sometimes what our strengths are *not*.
The person that thinks they're good at everything needs to read a different book that helps them understand reality. None of us are good at everything. Our superpowers are very interesting. Oftentimes, *we receive a lot of negative messages about them.*

For example, women, when they're little girls, if they have leadership skills, they may get told they're *bossy*. They might be told that they're mean, because little girls shouldn't be bossy. They don't hear, "Wow, look at those great leadership skills. Look at the great way she commands a room! And yes, we do need to work with her and make sure she's not steamrolling people. Nobody likes that. We need to make sure she's enrolling people positively along the way, because the best leaders don't bark orders at others, the best leaders enroll and influence the people around them to also be great leaders, in their own way.

Oftentimes we get mixed messages, and our interpretation is: *the way we are isn't okay.*
Some things we innately feel inside; things we want to rise up and do or be, we get told, "Oh, girls don't do that." Boys get told the same thing in different situations. For example, when boys have a lot of empathy, they might be told, "Man, you're soft" or "Stop that – you're acting like a girl." The Truth is (with a capital T!) that some men are very empathetic, that's one of their superpowers, which is a very loving, helpful relational skill.

The Gallup StrengthsFinders© model, with 40 years' of research, has come up with 34 strengths based on their assessment. It's a deep, amazing tool, because nobody has the same top five strengths. And, even if two people happened to have the same top five strengths, as Gallup calls it, the order in which your top five strengths show up won't match another's. But, even if they did, their lives would still look different because of being raised in different families, with different belief systems and life experiences. *All of those things come into play to create who you are and what you're good at.*

Regarding the stereotyping of superpowers, in the U.S., we over-genderize in an alarming way.

There are so many things that are not about gender that we try to make about gender.
Your superpowers have nothing to do with your gender. So, using the amazing superpower of empathy as the example, both men and women may have empathy in their top five strengths. It's a very compassionate strength, so oftentimes people with empathy enjoy being a nurse, caregiver, or counselor, and that could be a man or a woman. A similar thing occurs with leadership strengths, when a woman has *Command*, (which happens to be my number one strength). Command is a very "get it done" skill, and it's often widely misunderstood by both men and women, especially *when a woman has it.*

In contrast, when a man has command, it is considered a great, manly skill, necessary for CEOs, presidents, etc., and is even viewed as normal or politically correct in our culture. It's time to take a look at the *what's next* of leadership, the *what's next* in business, the *what's next* of politics, and in the relationships in our country. Let's get over the obsessive gender stereotyping... the O.G.S. I just made that up!

Let's also get over the race stereotyping. (Please, for the love of all that is holy...)
Let's get over the economic stereotyping. Everybody on the planet is born with unbelievable gifts and abilities, so it's important for us to just stop the judging, which we have all been guilty of, including me. *Let's all intentionally stop it.*

We deserve to interrupt those patterns that our cultures, families, jobs, churches, and friends have trained us to be limited by. That is all these attitudes do – limit.
The judgments and expectations that are so often wrong put people (including ourselves) in a box, and none of us belong in a box. None of us *want* to be in a box. In fact, we all want to blow up the freakin' box!

Our stories are so individualized and unique – in our upbringing, in all the different factors that make up each one of us. There are no two people exactly alike on this planet. No two people operate the same way. Isn't it astonishingly beautiful when we quit trying to make everybody act the way we think they should, and just let them be *them*?

I love these superpowers, because they have ZERO (nada, nothing) to do with gender.
It's simply about what you're exceptional at, about what you were born to do, and what you can get really, amazingly good at. *And, if you don't think that you have superpowers, you just don't know what they are yet.*

If you don't know them yet, it's time to unlock, ignite, and mobilize them in you.
Your superpowers are the things that will help you fulfill the mission(s) you feel compelled to do. So, not only do you need to learn what they are, you deserve to get coaching on them so they can be fully operational. Most people who learn their strengths, but don't get coaching, cannot even remember what they are, much less truly activate them at their highest levels.

What are some of the ways that my superpowers can be a weakness?

If I'm not using my strengths, that's a pretty big disadvantage.
Not only is not living in your strengths a personal disadvantage, but you're also withholding that special gift of who you are and of your abilities from the world. That means something positive is not happening…*because you're in the way of it.*

For example, dialing back your voice when you have a strength called *Input*, which is when a person likes to give and receive input and information. If you stuff your voice, you're doing a great disservice to yourself. *But, I would suggest you are also ripping off the rest of us, too.*

Stop holding back your voice. And, I will say this as a Life Success Coach, it's going to make you sick if you stuff your abilities and your talents. It can make you physically sick and emotionally sick, because that's not what you are designed to do – physically, emotionally, spiritually, and otherwise. And, it can even make your wallet sick, because you won't have the kinds of results and success long term that you need.

You're born the F-18 fighter jet. You were made to fly, and until you do, it's going to burn inside of you.
We can literally become unhealthy by denying ourselves, denying our true nature, and denying the thing that we were born to do. Our bodies are miraculous, and they give us feedback. It will give you feedback when you're not operating the way that you should. You will not feel well, and you will feel sick when you are not rising up to the things you should do. We know that about ourselves, and it's just like when we eat something bad. If you eat ten pounds of cotton candy, you're going to feel real sick, right? So, our bodies are feedback machines, tapping us persistently on the shoulder, and then if we don't listen, they will smack us across the face, and then put us in bed. And, if we still don't listen, we'll find ourselves in the hospital. How much will it take for you to pay attention? Your body will facilitate whatever it takes for you to get the message.

Tip: The better student you are to the signals that your body faithfully gives you, the sooner you're going to be operating at your highest and best levels, serving the world in a bolder way. So, we're not honoring our superpowers if we don't use them, and especially not if we deny them and push them down.

Also, if we misuse our strengths, they can show their "shadow" side.

I have great leadership and influencing strengths, like Command, Focus and Achiever. But, if I use that to try to over-control people, that's not good. Adolf Hitler may have had Command!

Controlling isn't leading. Controlling is an insecurity that is projected onto others. It's my attempt to desperately hold things together, because inside I feel like I am falling apart or not healthy. You can lead with command or other influential strengths by inspiring people, if they're willing. But, inspiring people means you need to be in *spirit* yourself. If you look at the word (inspire) itself, it comes from the inside, not the outside.

Contrast inspiration with control – control is trying to stimulate a response from someone, from the outside in. That's why it doesn't work well, or if it does, it doesn't leave them in a good space, it's not valuable, and it's not sustainable. Inspiring them is influencing them, enrolling a person by what inspires *them*, from the inside out. It's not *getting them to do what I want them to do*. It is finding out what makes them IGNITED, *and encouraging that so they're self-motivated to go.*

If you're misusing your superpowers, it can go to the shadow side, or show up like a weakness. If you're using them for the wrong reasons, if you're not being truthful, honest, or if what you are about is not positive, it will show up and make people not trust you. There have been many people in power in worldwide governments, in Hollywood, in business, in other organizations that are *not* using them with integrity. We need to use our superpowers and our strengths to stop people, organizations, or philosophies that are misusing their strengths and who are manipulating or abusing others.

The good news is, when people *are* living in their superpowers, when they're able to do their job in such a way that just absolutely unlocks every strength that they've got, allowing them to shine at the highest levels, that's when people create amazing results. *They can do this long-term and be fulfilled.*

If you find someone who doesn't love their job, they're either not in their strengths with that job, or they don't understand what their strengths are and haven't activated and fine-tuned them yet. This is a really important conversation when you're hiring or putting together any kind of team. It's not what you want them to be good at, not the gap you need filled and then hastily filling the gap with them. If you want them to be happy and great at what they do, then find out what fires them up and what fuels their passion, because that's what they're going to be really awesome at. Then, they will be an asset on your team. When people are thriving and successful at what they do, having confidence that they're doing a good job, creating a valuable difference, knowing their voice matters, then they're good for the people around them, too. *And, they will also be people that oftentimes will be able to weather the storms just like you.*

You don't want to waste your time, energy, and resources training someone that can never be great at what they do, and you don't want to be irresponsible and put just anybody in that role. At the end of the day, you know the job better than they do and the team that you're leading. If you understand these strengths and if you're tuned into these people, you're watching, you're paying attention and you're creating a safe work environment for people to give feedback and communicate. Then it becomes easy to see when people are in the wrong role, and that's a great time to make a strategic correction and put them in the right role.

Understanding your own gifts and making sure you're using them in a very balanced way (and to their maximum effectiveness) is not just about you understanding those strengths, *it's helping you understand the superpowers of others, too.*

One of my favorite workshops to do with any business, organization, or team is learning about strengths, because people love to learn to understand themselves. But, as people learn and begin to understand themselves better, they naturally start to understand others better as well. As we become more educated, our awareness then goes up.

As our awareness goes up, our judgment of others automatically begins to go down. That's what awareness and education do – they broaden our perspective. Knowing myself broadens and deepens my understanding, causing me to not be so narrow. I'm not so limited any longer. I'm not so ignorant. As my judgment goes down, my respect goes up; my respect for myself and my respect for other people's strengths even when they're very different from mine.

We tend to judge what we don't understand.
What we don't understand can make us nervous or afraid, but we don't have to be afraid of people who are different than us. We can be excited and encouraged about different gifts, and we can learn more about them to see how we can interact and to help one another. *It truly is a magic formula that makes things work.*

As my respect level goes up, conflict goes down, the challenges go down, fear and anxiety go down, effectiveness goes up, productivity goes up, the happiness factor goes up, and the *fun* goes up. YES!

Unlocking your own superpowers unlocks your ability to appreciate, love, respect, and trust others *in ways you probably didn't even understand existed.*
My husband took this assessment nine years after we were married. I won't say that I understand him completely now, but I understand him so much better! I wish I would have taken that assessment with him the moment I met him, but I'm grateful we took it as soon as we found out about it. It helped me understand him a great deal.

My husband has a superpower called *Harmony*. Harmony is wonderful, because people who have it just want people to be happy and to have a good time...all the time. Sometimes harmony people struggle to understand that people can't *always* have fun. We aren't always laughing and having a great time. It would be great, but it's not the way life works. People with harmony oftentimes avoid confrontation. They will run, hide, joke, and sometimes do anything to minimize or avoid confrontation. That can be very frustrating for those of us that like to tackle challenges and be proactive.

That used to be really hard for me. I like to see and take care of things before a conflict happens, but in contrast, he would prefer to slip away and hide from it. Inside I used to be judgmental about this. I didn't say anything necessarily to him, but to me, it used to seem like he was being irresponsible. Certainly there are times when we need to take responsibility and take things on, whether it's comfortable or not.

An "immature Harmony" can struggle with this shadow side of the strength. I don't know that anybody likes confrontation, but there are certain personalities that more naturally approach difficult issues with less anxiety or fear of them.

The profound part in all this for me was when I learned that his struggles around confrontation did not come from a bad place. They did not actually come from a weakness. Perceptions are not always correct, and mine certainly wasn't. Context changes everything. The context here was *strength*. The context was part of the beauty of him; the pure, innocent part of him. He truly wants people to be happy – he really does. He wants people to be having a good time...all the time. And, he does not always know how to navigate that, so it can come across as a negative thing.

It was huge for me to realize it was coming from a good place, although it still doesn't make it easy to deal with. Because of our different superpowers, oftentimes we still approach things pretty differently. Thankfully, my understanding went up as I was educated. My awareness also went up, and so my respect for him grew tremendously. At the same time, my judgment of him went down significantly, too.

Everyone has superpowers.
Everyone has a unique viewpoint, and it's relevant and valuable. We can all truly co-create a space with each other of unlocking our magic, harnessing our superpowers, and applying those strengths to make positive changes in the world.

Fuel for your flame:
Do you believe you have superpowers? If so, what might they be?
If you don't know, are you open to finding out?

Resource: Strengthsfinders 2.0© online assessment by Gallup

Chapter 3: Knowledge
by Terilee

Learn everything you can. Anytime you can. From anyone you can.
There will always come a time when you will be grateful you did.
~ Sarah Caldwell

It's always good to be learning, but there comes a time when you know
enough. Don't get stuck. Go! Do! ~Terilee Harrison

I continually seek opportunities for learning and growth. Do you?

The Message

As a leader, it is vital that you are always growing. It doesn't take a lot of effort to read or study 15 minutes a day. The key can be to have access to your study materials at all times. You never know when an appointment will be delayed and when you will have the opportunity to get your reading done.

During the months when I wrote my book *The Shameless Life*, I purposely did not read Brene Brown's work. Brene is a noted shame researcher and author. I did not want my book to be "Brene Jr's" thoughts. Instead, I researched shame in other places. Since my book has been complete, I have now read, studied, and taken notes of Dr. Brown's work. I love reading anything I can get my hands on about recovery and letting go of your past. In order to continue to help more people, I need to grow, daily.

What are some ways you can acquire more knowledge?
• Read more books.

Technology has changed how we can learn. You can read an actual paper book, listen to an audiobook (in the car or on the go) or read on any electronic device.

- Listen to podcasts or read blogs.

There are some amazing, weekly podcasts you can listen to or blogs you can read for inspiration and education as an entrepreneur. It's a great, quick way to keep plugged in. I enjoy Michael Hyatt's blog where he educates on building your platform, leadership, productivity, and more.

- Ask more questions.

Be curious. Don't be afraid of asking questions. Ask what you want to know from friends, colleagues, clients, experts – anyone you can.

- Build your network.

The more professionals I meet, the more I learn. I am a lot smarter now just from learning from my network. I live out the saying, "It's not what you know, it's *who* you know." Who do you know that you can ask for help or for them to share their experience and knowledge with you?

- Collaborate with others.

Let's face it, you cannot be good at everything. When you collaborate with others, you can glean from their expertise.

- Join a mastermind group.

A mastermind group is a group that meets periodically to brainstorm, hold each other accountable, and to grow together. You can glean a lot of knowledge when you participate in a high-level mastermind group. You also build solid relationships with high-level professionals. Sheli G and I met in a mastermind group!

- Listen more closely.

We all tend to talk too much. When I began learning how to be a coach, I discovered my listening skills needed some (okay, a lot of) improvement. Too often, do you find yourself listening to figure out how you are going to reply? When you listen more closely to people, you will learn more from them.

Danger. Danger.
It's easy to get caught up in the *I don't know enough's* and become paralyzed in taking action. You think you need to take one more course, hire one more coach, or attend one more conference. There is a strength called *Learner*. My husband's top strength is learner. Lucky for him, he is a teacher and minister, so he gets to study and present lessons all the time! Imagine a coach or a Realtor® who is a learner, though. It is especially easy for them to get caught thinking if they just had one more certification, *then* they will have enough knowledge to succeed. (But, when they finish, they will want just *one more* class...)

There comes a time when you need to trust yourself and step out. There comes a time when you *do* know enough. Perhaps that time is right now. *The only way to prove it to yourself is to take action!*

Fuel for your flame:
What can you read or study to gain more knowledge in your field?
What action can you take today to move forward, because you already know enough?

Chapter 4: Networking
by Terilee

Surround yourself with the dreamers and the doers, the believers and the thinkers, but most of all surround yourself with those who see the greatness in you. ~ Edmund Lee

I alone cannot change the world, but I can cast a stone across the water to create many ripples. ~ Mother Teresa

We're not born on an island, alone. We're born into community. Why? Because everything truly amazing happens when people collaborate together. ~ Sheli G

Have you ever signed up for an amazing business conference or joined a networking group and wondered how you can get the most out of it? I have, too. Here are some of the things I have learned during the many meetings I have attended over the last ten years.

The Message
What do you do before the event?
Is your message in alignment with who you really are? Let me tell you about my friend, Mike. When I first met him, he was selling life insurance. He was well liked by people he would meet while out networking, but when it came time to give his one minute commercial, it was a struggle for him. Why? Deep down, Mike didn't want to sell insurance. He really wanted to go back into Life Coaching and become a motivational speaker. Once he made the switch, it was night and day how he shined when he talked about what he did.

Do you feel like you shine when you talk about your work, or does it feel like a struggle? I have always found changes like these are best made *before* you join a group or attend a conference. Why spend more time (and money) promoting one message when you really want to promote a different one?

Do you have all the marketing materials you need?
I always keep business cards everywhere – my purse, my briefcase, and in my trunk! You never know when you will need them. If I have a large event or exhibit coming up, I begin preparing my marketing materials for my table weeks ahead.

Do you have a call to action?
I recommend you never network without a call to action. Here are some ideas: invite people you meet to opt-in to your email list, you can ask for speaking engagements, or perhaps invite others you meet to an upcoming event you are hosting. The most important thing is to move your business relationship forward!

When someone asks you, "What is your business?" Do you have an answer, or do you stammer and make something up at the last second? There have been times I have asked someone, "What do you do?" and they went on and on, not letting me get a word in. It is best to be prepared. People like to do business with people who can articulate what they do!

A template I have used for years is:
I _____ (action verb) my _____ (target market) with _____.

Here's an example of this for a financial advisor: "I help couples who own a home to become financially independent." Be specific in your answers to help you narrow your intentions and support clarity.

What do you do at the event?
Remember, it's never about you! Have you ever met a new person or reconnected with someone from the past, and they spent all their time talking about themselves, trying to convince you to buy their product? I hate that! In my networking efforts, I try to be all about the person I am speaking with. I ask myself, "How can I help them?" I want to be memorable (in a good way),

and I'm sure you do, too!

Quality not quantity.
I can recall being out networking with a friend at a business luncheon. We went our separate ways after we arrived and were both *working the room*. When she came back to the table, she stared in disbelief. I had collected three times as many business cards as she had. I told her not to consider it a failure if you don't come home with a TON of business cards. It is far better to make 2-3 excellent connections at every event than to come home just with a bunch of business cards.

Ask for what you need. You deserve it!
Have you ever wanted to meet a certain community leader? I tell everyone I speak with how this connection would help me. I have learned not to hesitate to ask. You never know who knows that person!

Divide and conquer. Attend with a Power Partner.
I prefer to attend networking events with a friend. I find it more productive and more fun! During networking time, I don't just talk to them. We usually split up to work the room. When I meet new people who will be a great connection for my friend, I bring them together and introduce them.

If possible, I schedule appointments to follow up with those I meet while still at the event. It is so much easier than trying to follow up with them once I arrive back at the office. I pull out my calendar and schedule time to follow up right on the spot. I either book a coffee appointment, plan to talk on Skype, or invite them to visit me at my office.

What do you do after the event?
I not only schedule time for the event on my calendar, but I also schedule follow up time, too. Within a day or two of the event, I mark off time on my calendar to reach out to those I met, even if it's just an hour.

Who can I develop a relationship with? Who can I do business with? Who can I refer to? I sort all the business cards I collected. Note: not everyone I meet will be someone I want to have a lifetime relationship with, but it helps if I reach out right away to those I do want to connect with.

I also request connections on social media so I can stay in touch. I have started making connecting on Facebook, LinkedIn, and Twitter part of my follow up.

I believe one of the most important factors in my networking habits is that I have grown to be confident that *I am enough* in my business to make connections who will help me fulfill my dreams. You are enough in your business, too!

That's it in a nutshell. Now go! Network! Connect!

Sheli G here, interrupting this networking chapter to bring you this: Don't *shotgun network* if you want to be positively remembered (or remembered at all). Terilee touched on this, too, but it's so important. Here I go...

Shotgun networking: Walking into a room and speed networking, such that you collect and give out a ton of cards. At the end of the day, you go home and have a stack-o-cards, yet you cannot remember who these souls are or why they matter. *And, believe me, they are doing the same thing with your card.*

Create positive energy when you walk into a room or event of any kind. Your body language, your clothing, your facial expressions, your carefully-chosen words, and how you show up in the one-on-one conversations you have will make you a lasting memory, and people will think to themselves; "Wow, I wish I knew more about him/her!"

Or, you always have the option to be a vanishing memory, and your time there can be wasted. A three-hour networking event where you have one to three meaningful, authentic conversations, and you can literally call them for coffee next week (and they will actually want to accept) is a home run. *Those are the cards worth trading for.*

Quality connections over massive card pushing = networking success.

Fuel for your flame:
What do you need to do before your next networking event?
What changes do you need to make in your follow up system after events?

Chapter 5: Follow Up
by Terilee

You have the fortitude within you to accomplish any goal you set your mind to. ~Terilee Harrison

All of our dreams can come true, if we have the courage to pursue them. ~ Walt Disney

It doesn't matter how great you start, if you fail to execute the follow up. BIG Results will only come to the ones who honor the whole process and don't abandon great leads along the way. ~ Sheli G

"The fortune is in the follow up." I've heard this saying over and over (for years!) But in the past, no matter what I wanted to accomplish in the outside, deep inside, I didn't believe in myself.

So what do you think happened?
- I was an excellent quitter.
- I didn't think I knew enough. I always thought I needed to sign up for another training.
- I majorly screwed up my follow up. I seemed to always have a big stack of business cards on my desk that I wasn't following up with in a meaningful way. In fact, I didn't have a Customer Retention Management system even set up.
- At the root of all this was this untruth: "I don't think that I deserved to make great money."

The Message
Can you relate with any of those thoughts or outcomes?

There have been two things that have helped me increase my follow up and create better results:

1. Acknowledging and letting go of my past.
I was always good at investing in my business, but I did not take

time to work on *me*. I was missing out on the fact that personal growth and development is a lifetime journey. Once I began working on me, I found it was almost like peeling back the layers of an onion. Once I dealt with the big stuff, over time I was able to work on other stuff as it comes up. Have you invested in yourself? If you want to create better results through more effective follow up, I recommend you start within!

2. Learning and understanding that we all have "competing commitments."
Why didn't I ever do what I said I was going to do? I didn't understand that no matter what goal I wanted to accomplish, I always had my inner game competing with my outer game.

How many times have I wanted to lose (the same) 20 pounds? My "outside game" would say, "I am going to lose 20 pounds in two months!"

But my inner game would go on and on saying things like:
"You don't deserve to be thinner."
"You aren't a winner."
"You will never be disciplined enough to make that happen!"
"You haven't weighed that much in 20 years. How do you think you can accomplish this now?"

Did I lose the 20 pounds? Most times, I didn't! Before I knew it, I would start cheating on my food program and skip out on some of my exercise because my inner game was competing with my outer game!

To overcome this, I have learned to set a reward or a penalty. It's got to be a reward SO big that I can't stand myself. I've got to do *everything* possible to accomplish my goal.

I have learned I am personally motivated by setting a penalty. I have accomplished *more* by setting penalties for myself over the last three years than I had in the ten years prior. The most effective penalty you set has to be *painful*. Penalties are always personal. What's painful for me might not be painful for you.

My bikini bet.
The first time I set a penalty, I was at a meeting with 250+ entrepreneurs. I committed in front of them that I wanted to lose 30 lbs. in 90 days. At the time, this would have been a challenge for me. In front of this entire group, I was asked to set a penalty. What would I have to do if I did not lose 30 lbs. in 90 days? I committed to the crowd if I did not reach my goal, I would model a bikini on the first Wednesday after the 90 days were over at my Diamond Bar (CA) team meeting. I picked this because most of the members were in attendance that night. Here's the deal: I have *never* worn a bikini – even when I was young and looked TOTALLY amazing. There was *no* way I was going to model a bikini at a business meeting! That would have been excruciating!

So what do you think happened? I actually lost 37 lbs. in 40 days and kept it off. I did not cheat once during that time, because I would tell myself, "I'm not wearing a bikini!" whenever I would even think about cheating. It was the first time I learned I am greatly motivated by setting a penalty.

Here's another example:
I don't even do my own laundry. My husband does. In order to complete a coaching certification by a certain date, I set a penalty that I would do my friend, Nancy's laundry every week for four weeks, and she has a lot of laundry! I did *everything* it took to reach that goal. There was *no way* I was going to do her laundry for four weeks!

Once you have worked on the conversation with your inner game and you are ready to successfully manage your follow up once and for all, here are some practical tips to get you started:

- Be organized. You've got to have your act together. Period.

- Manage your data. Enter and update your contacts. Keep a calendar. Use a planner.
- Set up a follow up system and stick to it.
- Ask for the help you need. Maybe a Virtual Assistant or a Strategy Coach.
- Use a great CRM. There are great customer retention management systems out there. Pick one and use it. There's Aweber, MailChimp, and Infusionsoft, just to name a few.

Fuel for your flame:

What can you do to be more effective in your follow up?
What is a penalty you could set for yourself, for your next goal, that would help your inner game compete with your outer game?
And/or, what is a reward that you could treat yourself to upon achieving your follow up goals?
What really motivates you?

Chapter 6: Feedback
by Sheli G

When one person says it, it's an opinion. When you hear it again, and again, it may be something to listen to. ~ Sheli G

I've learned that people will forget what you said, people will forget what you did, but people will never forget how you made them feel.
~ Maya Angelou

We can't know what we don't know until we know it, and then once we know it, we cannot NOT know it unless we choose to deny it. ~ Sheli G

It's really naïve and ignorant to think our inner thoughts and what we are really *about* as a person does not translate. Everybody around you automatically gets it.

We've all been there.
I've been the person who was more the taker than the giver. I've been in a situation, just like you, where I was out mostly for myself; for my agenda, my goals. I did it a lot when I was younger, not being very wise in business. I wanted to see what I could do and what I could create. I wanted to test my limits and capabilities. It seemed normal at that time, and everyone was doing it. *I was not very self-aware.*

My ideas and visions were very important to me.
I did not consider everybody else around me as much as I should have and as much as I needed to. It took some hard lessons because people did not always sense my heart. I wasn't always operating from, or showing, my heart.

People used to say, "Wow, when I first met you, I just didn't really get you. You seemed so hardcore and pretty self-absorbed." In my 20s, it was hard to hear comments like that, because I knew I wasn't that person inside. *Geez, really? I don't want people to think of me that way. My intentions are good, and yeah, I want to scale up in business, make money and do all of those things, but I don't want to hurt or offend anybody to get there. I don't want anybody to think I'm a bad person. I don't want people to feel steamrolled like they're not important.*

I had to learn that I was somehow sending out those communication signals. And, if people are responding to you in a way that you think is counter to your true message and how you think you are showing up, it's time to listen and consider the feedback. *Ponder whether your message is really your message.*

The Message

Hopefully you're open to receive constructive feedback. People won't give you feedback if you're too egotistical, if you never slow down, if you don't listen, or if you are not approachable. Why would they stop and spend their valuable time and energy to have a confrontation with you if you're just going to get mad and steamroll them, or if you're not going to listen or care?

People are only going to give you compassionate feedback about the 360 perspective of you, if you're approachable, if you stop sometimes, and if you get quiet and listen.
If you really want to know what people think about you, and be the greatest leader in the universe, you will stop and listen to the feedback *even when it's hard.* You will listen to the feedback even when you don't agree in that moment, and when your insides want to be defensive and shut down, you will choose to stay in the conversation. You will let it come in, and you will think about it and consider it very intentionally for a period of time (not automatically dismissing it).

Some of the worst leaders today are those who don't stop and open themselves up for feedback. They think they know everything and none of the rest of us know anything. Or, they hear feedback and just blow it off, because they think they have the corner on every answer and every idea, denying any other data. That's really sad. At the end of the day, they're causing pain. They'll hurt people along the way, yes, but ultimately they hurt themselves the most by not growing to be that great leader they were meant to be. They cannot be the *what's next* in leadership – the ignited leader and *The Ignited Entrepreneur*.

Sometimes feedback comes to you compassionately, and people articulate it well. Sometimes they will blast you.
People sometimes rip your face off with their feedback. I've been the recipient of that, but I sometimes needed it, too. There were times I did not know what I did not know. We can't know what we don't know until we know it...and then once we know it, we cannot un-know it, *unless we just want to deny it.*

The feedback in my early years of being an entrepreneur (in my 20s) was, at times, both devastating and very hurtful to hear, and sometimes it made me mad.
Until we can stop and see the areas we need to grow in, and even some of the areas where we really stink, we can't fix it. If we're not aware, we can't be better, we can't grow, or evolve. We can't go find the resources, mentors, and solutions to scaling in those areas *if we don't even admit that we have blind spots.*

The early feedback I received as an entrepreneur was one of the absolute best gifts I could have been given. The people that gave me feedback, both the people that gave it to me compassionately and some of the people that weren't very compassionate, *they all helped me. I am eternally grateful.*

And, like you, I've been judged wrongfully at times, too.
I've been told things about my character and intentions that flat out weren't true. But, I'm not talking about that. I'm talking about taking all the feedback into consideration and finding "themes." After one person said it, I thought it was a random opinion. But, when different people from different places and spaces, are all giving you similar kinds of feedback...you can start to say, *wow, what is the common denominator of these things?*

Why does this keep coming back to me like a bad boomerang? And, that common denominator was, in fact, me. *Or, you.*

The truth is, if I really want to grow, learn and be the absolute best I can be as a human being, as a mom, as a business owner, as a philanthropist, or whatever my causes and dreams are, I get to learn how to listen to feedback. Feedback and me: a partnership that will make me the best that I can be. That's the kind of collaboration that refines you and brings out miraculous leadership in you. We can be the *what's next* of leadership today.

If you are willing, be open and ask for feedback, but here's what I would say about that. *Be willing to receive it, because if you really create a safe place for people, they'll give you feedback.*

When they give you feedback, honor it.
They may be truth nuggets that help you uncover the treasure chest of your leadership, and it can't happen unless you mine the gold in those honest conversations.

Fuel For Your Flame:
On a scale from 1-10, how well do you take feedback? (1 being not at all, 10 being perfectly)
Make a few notes about how you have grown from feedback that was given to you, that you heard.

Chapter 7: Market by Terilee

If you build it, post it, like it, share it, pin it and tweet it, they will come. ~ Unknown

Marketing yourself is not prideful. Thinking that your business will survive without it, is. ~ Sheli G

The Message

Marketing is an integral part of all business success. In order to love you and buy your product, people have to know about you. The first question you always have to ask is: Who are you marketing to?

Who is your target market?

Over the years, I have heard some amazing Mary Kay friends say, "Anyone with skin is a good referral for me." Yes, but there's more. Successful marketers narrow it down and know exactly who their target market is.

_____ Sex
_____ Age
_____ Marital Status
_____ Number of children
_____ Faith
_____ Income
_____ Education Completed
_____ Career
_____ Geographical Location

Several years ago, I co-hosted Elevate Radio with my amazing friend, Marlia Cochran. When we were planning our show and before we did our branding, we got specific about our target market. We got so specific that we named her "Melissa."

Whenever we had a question about the direction of the show, we would ask, "Does this pertain to Melissa?" or, "Is this what Melissa needs to hear?"

What is your message?
1. The first step to define your message is to create an elevator pitch that's unique, and off the charts. It should get them to ask you, "Tell me more!"
2. I "action verb" "target market" with "benefits of working with you."
3. Action verb: help, teach, assist, train, provide, etc.
4. Target market: Who did you narrow down to above? Men and women, women, married couples, families, at-risk youth, entrepreneurs, preschoolers, etc.
5. Make a list of all the benefits of working with you. Some of mine are:
    a. Have a fresh start.
    b. Feel more confident.
    a. Experience freedom to love themselves and others.
    c. Once you have this list, pick your top three.

Fuel for your flame:
Who is your target market?
What are a couple of marketing ideas you can begin to strategize on today?

Chapter 8: Future
by Sheli G

The thing about your future is, it is made up of powerful moments, starting RIGHT NOW. Let us begin! ~ Sheli G

Too many of us are not living our dreams because we are living our fears. ~ Les Brown

It was liberating to finally realize that I'm totally vincible. I have weak moments or days, I'm going to make mistakes, I'm going to fall flat on my face, and sometimes when I do it, I will do it in front of everyone…because I go big. ~ Sheli G

The future is something that many of us think about so often, don't we? People think about the future: planning the future or expecting and envisioning what their future might look like. I also find in my coaching and consulting practice that people are often thinking about their past, both the great victories and amazing moments that they can remember, and maybe even more often, about their mistakes and failures.

The Message

We do vision boards, and we write goals. We strategically plan. In fact, you usually can't start a business without some sort of business plan. Whether it's in your head or on paper, start vetting through it more officially. If you want a business loan or partnerships, a business plan is a must.

The future is actually made of moments…starting with right now! Because the future is made up of the decisions I make in this moment. The good news is, whatever I choose in this moment, *I have a new choice five minutes from now.*

The future is made up of my mindset in this moment.
The future requires planning and preparation, which is critical and paramount to getting great results. Most successful leaders that you sit down and talk to, however you define success, you'll find that they did a lot of planning, preparation, goal setting, milestone counting, looking at what works, and looking at what doesn't work, and then planning again for the future.

The challenge is, none of us have a crystal ball. Many times, life looks nothing like our hopeful, and sometimes fairly naive expectations. Sometimes life looks way better than anything we could have imagined!

I personally quit trying to tell the future a long time ago.
It doesn't mean I quit setting goals. I've got to know where I'm at and where I'm headed, or I'm random like a shotgun going off in different directions, hoping it'll land on something good. That generally doesn't work. But, keep in mind that having a plan, goals, and milestones are all forms of *expectation. For me, I will plan, AND I've learned to be willing to simultaneously let go as well, and adapt to what IS.*

The future is going to look like what it does, based on the evolution of events that we have yet to know about.

When I was in the mortgage business, I used to get asked that fateful question, "Should I lock in my interest rate or not?" In other words, what is this market going to do, is it going up or down? I got to the point where I realized, I'm not God, and I think he's the only one that truly knows what this market is going to do! After a while I started telling people, "I don't have a crystal ball. It broke a long time ago. You'll have to decide if you want to lock or not, because I just don't know." #Empowering

We just do not know what the future is going to bring. We can't control that. We can't control culture, economy, people, technology or trends.
When I was growing up, we didn't know Facebook was going to

exist. I didn't know we'd all be on cell phones. I didn't know I'd be writing a book. I do the right planning and preparation now, I stay positive, I keep dialing up my strengths, dialing up my resources, serving people in the highest way possible, doing what I'm called to do, facilitating moment by moment, from the smallest nudge that I feel, to the greatest move that I need to make...and *the future becomes what it should be.*

There are challenges that will no doubt come, and there is also bliss that is coming. There are some joyful moments that end up better than what you could ever imagine, if you're open, if you're willing, and if you stay the course. If you do your work, even when nobody is watching. If you do the right thing, and you're a good steward of your time, your energy, your thoughts, and your servanthood. And, you do that even in the dark when nobody's looking. Do that even when you're feeling mis-understood. It matters, and joy comes.

Do the work even when it's hard.
It's easy to do those things when it's easy. When things are going your way and you're feeling good, when your health is good and the sun is out...sometimes those are the ideal times to go out there, get it done, and make it happen, consistently. It's easy *then*, to be a highly-committed, Ignited Entrepreneur; to be that ignited leader we expect ourselves to show up as. At the end of the day, for most true entrepreneurs, no one can have higher dreams and expectations of us than us.

There came a point in my personal and spiritual development that I realized it wasn't everyone around me putting all the expectations and pressure on me. Although, people can and will try to do that. But I was actually teaching and training the people around me what to expect from me. I expected so much for myself. I expected supernatural results, day after day, month after month, and year after year. *It was a lot of pressure.*

I modeled to my circles to treat me like I was invincible, because that's the way I was acting and showing up.

It was a pretty liberating moment when I realized *I am totally vincible.*
I have weak moments or days. I'm going to make mistakes. A lot. I'm going to fall flat on my face, and sometimes when I do, I will do it in front of everyone…because **I go big,** just like many of you. #EpicFails

I cannot control the future, but if I do everything in my power to make the future what it's supposed to be, and the best that it can be, *I have to start living in this moment right here, right now.*

What are my thoughts? What are my actions from the tiniest to the biggest? What are my conversations? What am I surrounding myself with? Who are the people I surround myself with? What are the books, the movies, the sights, sounds? What food am I putting into my body? What dreams and hopes and aspirations do I cultivate? How do I kick the negative thoughts and images to the curb? Sometimes those things hijack your brain, entering in from random places, like a billboard or something somebody says, but we don't have to hang onto them. We have the choice to refuse to rent them a room in our head and spirit.

The past is wonderful, because it is your great teacher, your mentor. *The past is an amazing vault of experiences, files, people, relationships and things that give you so much knowledge, understanding and discernment to do what you need to do today.*

You also need and deserve to move beyond the successes of your past, because you're not there anymore. Celebrating is super important. Having intentional, sacred ceremony around the stunning success moments, achievements and milestones of our lives, and teaching our kids to do the same thing is <u>huge</u>. *Don't just move on to the next thing and go, go, go and do, do, do more.* That's an American Disease. #GoDoSyndrome

Sometimes, the value is not in getting to the next 20 things on your list that day. It's in stopping and taking a deep breath and saying, "Wow, that was amazing. I went for that goal or milestone, or I served in that way, and look at the blessing that's coming back. Look at the great result. Look at the fruit from the labor that's coming from the vine. I am blessed!"

But, at a certain point fruit dies. We pick it, we eat it, it's gone, and we need to plant more trees that produce more shade and fresh fruit. We need to keep creating, cultivating, evolving, and adapting, *so that we can create the future that we say we want.*

Have you ever noticed how easy it is to talk about the future?
It's easy to say, "Oh, I want a Ferrari," or "I want the vacation house in Paris!" "I want to build an orphanage!" or "I want the beach place in the summertime." "I want to be debt-free." "I want to pay off my Mom's home." Those are wonderful things, and it's really easy to have those scripts we chant or write down, and yet not be intimately connected with those goals right here, right now, in this moment. Have the goal *and* say, "If that's really true that I want to pay off my Mom's house, what is it going to take to do that?" Then, break it down into bite size steps I can metabolize and that my team can metabolize, so that we don't get stuck in the overwhelm of, *oh my gosh, oh my gosh, we want this huge thing, but we don't see how to get there!*

Your future is being made out of these micro moments right now, as you read these very words. What are you creating? What do you see that you want and do you really want that? Do you really, really want that? In the depths of your soul? Not just what you tell people, not just what you've been trained to think, or what you think you should say.

What is your *why*? Why do you want to start that business? Why are you so passionate about that cause? Why do you want to invent that thing or compose that song? *What positive value is it going to bring to you, your family, your community, your town, your country, and just maybe to the planet?*

Things are only impossible until they're done. And...

It's going to take a lot of work.
If you're not a hard worker, ongoing and consistently, you deserve to learn how to be. We're all raised in different families with different environments, and some of that is definitely out of our control. But, people can learn habits and behaviors. We can learn how to work hard. We can learn systems, platforms, and applications that help us work harder, smarter, more efficiently, and effectively. Not that you won't have moments where you struggle or even lack clarity and say, "Who am I, and why did I decide to do this ridiculous thing anyway?!"

We all have those emotional moments. It's good to have a moment like that and question yourself, "Is this really what I do want? I thought it was. But, is it still?" You're going to come up with your answer. And, your answer, if it's really the right thing, time and all of that, will be YES. Yes keep going. Yes, sometimes it's hard, but it will be worth it. *Do it anyway.*

There will be days you feel like quitting. Welcome to the human race! Welcome to being normal!
Everybody feels like quitting some days. Everybody just wants to go run to the nearest cave, and pull the covers over their head sometimes, or just sit around and watch movies, play video games, eat ice cream, *or whatever it is you like to do to escape or even self-medicate.*

Find people that can give you real perspective.
Find people that will help you get back on track. *We don't get screwed up alone, and we don't get well alone.* We don't succeed alone, either. Get the resources, tools, support, and the people that you need to get re-inspired, re-ignited, educated, healthy, or whatever it is that you need.

It's not going to be easy, and that's why not everybody does it.
It's not going to be easy, and that's why some people fail. And some people fail all the way up until the point at which they succeed, because they're learning, growing, developing, fine-tuning and honing, and then they knock it out of the park. Those amazing stepping-stones are absolutely necessary to go where we intend to go.

We need people that have succeeded ahead of us, people that we respect, that we admire, people that have had the highs and the lows that we need to tap into their pool of knowledge, the wellspring of their wisdom, just to make our path a little bit more smooth, a little bit more objective, a little more reasonable.

Your future is going to be fantastic, based on the choices you make right now. The future is going to be incredible, if you choose. The biggest thing to know is we're *at choice*. We were at choice yesterday. We're at choice right now, and we will be at choice tomorrow. *If you make mistakes, own your mistakes!*

Be accountable. Be responsible.
You can't fix, change, or be better if you don't acknowledge what's not working. As much as we want to celebrate victories and successes, we also want to be really clear of what's not working, what's out of alignment, what needs to be tweaked, or changed. We need to know when something's obsolete, when it's old school, when it's antiquated. We deserve to continue to grow and evolve at the rapid rate that an Ignited Entrepreneur deserves to, to not only stay up with the marketplace that we're in, but to be the *what's next*.

Are you willing to be the *what's next* that we so badly need in our future, for our children and for our grandchildren?
Whether they're of our bloodline or not, they're all our children, because we all belong to each other. So, what are you doing to set up the future and make it better, even if it is just for one person? When your loved ones have a memorial service for you one day,

and they celebrate your successes, your philosophies, the messages that are left behind, the funny stories, what are they going to miss about you?

What legacy do you want to leave?
If you were to pass on today, what legacy would you leave? Have you made the difference that you want to make? Because each one of us absolutely can, and each one of us do, in some way, somehow.

What are they going to gather around and say about you? What are they going to remember about you? If they were to say, "These are the top two or three things that I remember about Sheli," what would they say? Would they say she was a giver, or a taker? Would they say that she moved in spite of her fear, or would they say that she stayed trapped by insecurity and doubt? Would they say that she helped other people think about what they want, and possibilities, and maybe be a small part of their evolution towards their successes, and realizing their dreams?

Imagine when your friends and family gather at your memorial service and say, "Wow, he blazed a trail so that I could come behind and be my highest and best self. He lived out what he said that he believed in. He didn't just talk about it. He meant it. He was the same person when nobody was looking or if you were talking to him one-on-one at the coffee shop. He gave to the least of these, even to those who could do nothing in return for him. He laughed. He cried. He lived out his calling, and he left it all on the floor. He didn't leave any amount of energy inside of himself untapped."

There are inventions yet to be invented. There are songs yet to be written, and books! You have a book in you! In fact, you probably have ten. There are games we have yet to play. There are children that are yet to be born, that are going to come behind us and change the world, too. And why shouldn't all of us be right in the middle of that? Because I know you. You're reading this book because you want to grow. *You're reading this book because something inside of you is on fire.*

You're reading this book because you're just wanting a little more confirmation, information, inspiration, and affirmation. And, if you're looking for a sign, you've just found it.

Some of you are reading this, and it causes a visceral reaction inside of you right now. There's an emotional response. It's saying "Yes, I get it! I'm the one! I'm the next leader, the next Ignited Entrepreneur. I'm going to let that fire that is deep inside of me out. I'm going to let it kindle, burn, grow, and be a passion that is unstoppable! There is no lie that can stop me. There is no abuse. There is no bad news. There is nothing, NO thing, that's going to get in the way of my purpose, because I am the next Ignited Entrepreneur. I am joining the ranks, and together we will positively ignite the planet."

Fuel for your flame:

What are you learning about your future, right now?

What intentional or courageous step do you need to and are you willing to take to step into your future, starting with this moment?

The Ignited Entrepreneur
Cultivates Well Being

Well-being is paramount to The Ignited Entrepreneur. To both succeed, and to sustain. Wellness is individualized, based on our own core values and criteria. It is foundational to establish your plan and intention for your overall Wellness. ~ Sheli G

Chapter 9: You
by Terilee

Today you are You, that is truer than true. There is no one alive who is Youer than You. ~ Dr. Seuss

Take responsibility for your Destiny. Be accountable for your Legacy. The world needs YOU. We need you. ~ Sheli G

The world needs you, and it needs your story. The world isn't the same without the real you showing up. ~ Terilee Harrison

(We wrote those quotes without any collaborating. Your writers are so on the same page!)

We do business with those we know, like (or love), and trust. But, the majority of the business people we meet are showing up as who they think *you* want them to be. They want to make sure you like them. So, who is it you are really doing business with?

I know this to be true because I have lived this life. I now am so much more open about who I really am and where I have been on my journey. Even so, I can recall *losing sleep* because I was so worried about letting people know the real me.

The Message

Right after my husband, Terry, and I moved to our current home, I had an opportunity to speak at the annual Ladies' Day at our church. Terry is the minister there. We hadn't lived there long, and even though I was in the process of writing my book, *The Shameless Life*, at the time (which tells *all* of my story) these women still didn't know very much about me and my past. I remember in the weeks leading up to the event, there were several times I would lay awake for hours at night worrying, "What will happen if I tell them who I really am? Will they accept me? Will Terry get in trouble because of my past?" And, it wasn't just the lying awake at night. The week leading up to the event, there were several days when Terry and I had lunch together. I can remember telling him several times at lunch that week, "I just don't want to get you fired!"

What do you think happened after I spoke that day? Was there a lynching? Did he get in trouble? Far from it. I had blown the possibilities all out of proportion. You see, I only received love and acceptance that day. Much to my surprise, they just loved me *more*.

There is a gift that is available to each and every one of us, if we are willing to take it.
This is the extraordinary gift of being loved for who you really are. Should you wish to receive this gift, all that is asked in return is for you to *be willing to share the gift of who you truly are to the world.*

I have been in conversations with businessmen who have told me about their past life in gangs on the street or how they spent time in prison. I have talked with businesswomen who danced in strip clubs. I could go on and on. When these beautiful souls trusted me with the precious gift of who they really were, I simply loved and accepted them.

Have you ever kept the truth of who you are from the people in your life? Have you ever worried they would not accept you if they really knew you? First, what is the truth of who you are?

The truth is:
You are extraordinarily Beautiful.
You are Unique. You are Loved.
You are Special. You are Important.
You are Strong.
You are Empowered.

Sheli G here...parachuting in on Terilee's chapter. I wanted to comment here because this chapter is about YOU. Because I am a coach/consultant, *you* are my favorite topic. What are your dreams, goals, desires, callings, mission, purpose, passion? Are you fulfilled in work, personally, relationally? What is in the way if you are not? Your past? Obstacles? Fear? Friends and family that don't believe in you? One thing that we can control, in spite of our circumstances is ourselves. *Even in weird, challenging, or tragic times, I am driving me: my reactions to others, my decisions, and the way I move through and past my circumstance.*

I love the story of one of my heroes that I have never met, but he is on my "Board of Directors" anyway. By the way, my board of directors are the legacy leaders from history or my life that I base a lot of my "I want to be like them when I grow up" on. MLK Jr., Mother Teresa, Les Brown, and many more are on my board.

Nelson Mandela:
Most of you know his name, and possibly part of his epic story. He shined a light not only for himself, but he lit a path of *hope* and *freedom* for countless others. Is there anything most of us want more than Hope and Freedom?

At one point, Nelson was captured and wrongfully imprisoned after the apartheid government labelled him a terrorist. In the winter of 1964, Nelson Mandela arrived on Robben Island, where he would spend 18 of his 27 prison years. In his tiny cell, the hard floor his bed, a bucket for his toilet, he was forced to do hard labor.

One time per year he was allowed one visitor, for only 30 minutes. Every six months, he could write and receive only one letter. I have had my dark moments, my "dragons" to slay if you will, and yet I cannot imagine this sentence! Maybe you have had a "prison" that you have dealt with in your life on some level, where you can relate. Or, maybe you've had a dark time when perhaps you thought, "I cannot make it through this, it's too hard and the road, too long."

Here are just a few remarkable, miraculous highLIGHTS of Nelson Mandela's courageous story.

Neville Alexander was one of the "young revolutionaries" sent to Robben Island as a prisoner, almost a year after Mandela. Mandela and his comrades warned the hotheaded young soldiers, saying essentially, "Guys, you are going to kill yourselves if you act like this. These guards will give you barely enough food to survive, if you're lucky, and they will punish and torture you until you break, collapse, and give in. The worst part about all of that if it happens, is that you won't have gained anything from imprisonment, whereas we can actually learn, achieve, and gain something from this experience. #wow

The young soldiers at first were too angry, and shocked at this objective approach to immediately metabolize it. Yet, Nelson was so grounded in what they were creating, inside these unthinkably dark prison walls, that soon they were all following his lead, being polite and obedient, yet speaking their truth with respect and dignity.

Amidst his son dying while he was on the island, and amidst mass rumors that Winnie, his wife, was cheating on him (the newspaper clippings were strategically placed under his cell door), Nelson remained a man steadfast in his character, his leadership, and his transparency. He would call some of the men in his close circle into his room at times to share his heart, as the burdens were so great. Even through all that, his focus was on the collective, on creating good and light in the darkest place on earth...astounding.

He had no proof that he would ever get out. He had no crystal ball telling him that someday he would be lifted up as one of the world's *greatest* heroes, ever. He had no guarantee he would even survive, as that was a daily question for them all. But, he took a stand in his darkest hour, for himself and for his tribe at that time, and for his core beliefs, that all should be treated equally with love and compassion. He allowed the light of his inner strength and commitment to carry on his life's great work no matter where, how, or what obstacle and enemy he encountered.

He was unwaveringly committed, passionate, and consistent in his relentless pursuit to leave every place and soul better than he found them. He was a victim of imprisonment, yet he chose to not be victimized. It was a corrupt system, but he interrupted, disrupted, and changed that system from inside the belly of the beast. His example, his modeling of strength, purpose, and hope saved countless lives. Not just physically, but psychologically, spiritually, and emotionally.

He demonstrated that no matter what, regardless of how hard it gets, even amidst every obstacle and pain imaginable, you can stand in WHO YOU ARE, in what you believe and what God has called you to do. No excuses.

From Prisoner to President.
Now, is there anything you can't do, overcome and create, if you

are called to it? YOU have that resilience inside of you. YOU have people that are waiting for you to rise up, or rise up even more, and lead. YOU have a message, a story, a product, a service and an answer for those who you are called to help.

I wish I could meet each of you – no kidding. (Terilee will back me up on that one!) I wish I could tell you this in person. I believe it with every cell in my body. You were born for greatness, and to create your own miracles of work, service and relationship. Unlock yourself, however that unfolds for you. Take responsibility for your destiny. Be accountable for your legacy. The world needs YOU. We need you.

When is the last time someone told you the truth? When is the last time you reminded yourself of this truth? Too often, it's the negative things you are told in life that stick with you. You replace them as truth, and it becomes what you tell yourself over and over. *I think it's a great time for a truth check.*

Fuel for your flame:
Is there something about yourself you would love to share with the world, but haven't yet?
What is one step can you take today to begin offering your extraordinary gift to others?

Chapter 10: Mindset
by Sheli G

Your mindset is your most precious commodity. Cultivate, feed, protect and nurture it like your mindspace is a literal gold mine, because it is.
~ Sheli G

The most common way people give up their power is by thinking they don't have any. ~ Alice Walker

Manifesting starts in the mind. A thought begins like a seed planted. Then we speak into that thought giving it a voice, sound. The seed sprouts. Then, we begin to act on that voice, that proclamation of what is to come. The plant begins to grow. Then our actions begin to get bigger, involving others. The idea matures. We bear fruit. ~ Sheli G

Your Mindset. This is such an important foundation to anything you want to succeed at professionally, as well as personally. It's all in the mindset. In real terms, what does that mean?

The Message
Mindset by definition according to TheFreeDictionary.com:
A habitual or characteristic mental attitude that determines how you will interpret and respond to situations. Mentality, mindset, outlook. Attitude, mental attitude – a complex mental state involving beliefs and feelings and values and dispositions to act in certain ways; "he had the attitude that work was fun."

Henry Ford simplified mindset really well with his quote; "Whether you think you can or can't, you're right."

Where do we get our mindset from? In working with people on a deep level over the last 20 years, here is what I have determined:
- Genetics
- Culture including geographical location, community, religion, business, gender biases, networks etc.

- Family dynamics
- Life Experiences
- Core Beliefs
- Mentors
- Our Core Network including family, and closest personal friends and professional associates
- What stimulus we listen to, read and otherwise let into our minds and spirits
- Education including schooling, reading, classes, seminars, trainings etc.
- Strengths
- Health including physical, mental, relational and spiritual

After reading that list, some of you may be feeling great, knowing that your mindset is exactly where it needs to be, based on those contributors. Some of you may be frustrated and fearful, thinking that some of those factors have not set you up for your highest levels of success. And still others of you may be sitting there thinking, "I don't have a freakin' clue what my mindset is?!" Wherever you are, it's all good, because when you know where you are, you can go from there and scale, always and in all ways. Positive and productive mindset takes time, intentionality and awareness of how to have the best mindset to accomplish your goals and dreams.

At the end of this chapter, there are a few questions to give you an idea where you are at. *Take the time to honestly evaluate yourself.*

Here's the good news: Mindset is created by the above contributors, and can be dialed **UP** as you change those dynamics. There is a choice. You can evolve and upgrade your mindset. Yes!

For example, when you get physically healthy with regular exercise, and you eat healthy Organic foods, your energy level goes up, in your physical stamina as well as mental alertness, for more hours in the day. Your days of being sick are greatly reduced or go away. Does this affect your mindset? Absolutely. Consider having one, two, three or more hours in the day where you are not only awake, but *fully* energized and mobilized either at work, home or both. What do you think you could create and contribute in those hours?

Your mindset is affected by your network.
You cannot choose your family that already exists, but the good news is, you *can* decide how much time you spend with them, where, and why. If there are negative influences in your family, limit your availability to them. Just because they are your family doesn't mean they are healthy, safe or a good space for you to hang out in. Sometimes the terrorist in our lives is a relative. *This sucks, but you don't have to stay hostage to them.*

In your friendships you have every freedom to choose who you spend time with, how much time, and where. This is critical for you to take responsibility of, and to choose to support yourself with safe, positive people that challenge you, and inspire you.

Are your friends positive? Healthy? Goal driven? Successful? If not, quit letting them drain your precious energy! Quit enabling them. Quit complaining about them, and do something about it (ouch). But, it's true. You control that part of your network, and *it can make a huge difference, if not change everything.* Here is another interesting aspect; when you get out of toxic relationships, then the other person also has an opportunity to grow and learn if they so choose. *Sometimes, when we stay after the expiration date of a relationship or event, we are just in the way for them, too. It's not just about us, after all.*

In your professional network there are many layers of players. You have partners, investors, employees, affiliates, vendors, clients, etc., but you also have extended collaborations with unlimited professionals both live and online with social platforms, associations, clubs, groups, etc. *Choose wisely.* Someone once said "You become like the five people you spend the most time with." Would you agree?

When I am around a negative person for any period of time, I feel more negative and very limited.
It's a restrictive space, usually coming from a root of fear-based living. Not fun! Not a place where ideating, dreaming and goal setting can be cultivated easily. It's like putting our dream in the ring with a massive, black, dark dragon-like opponent... breathing fire on us. That is not fuel for your flame. That is the melting of your brain, and spirit. Try to be productive, positive, and visionary in that space. It's a tough if not impossible set up.

When I am around the doers, the dreamers, the risk takers, the achievers, the lovers, the courageous ones...I do more of all of that. Don't you?
These kinds of inspirational people usually come from a place of service, vision, love and community. *What do you want to create?*

There are some very basic "Rules of Manifesting" what you say that you want:
1. First: We become open to a thought.
2. Next: We have one or more thoughts.
3. Then: We decide we are going to act on a specific thought, and take a step.
4. Next: We take a step forward based on the thought that now becomes a goal or target, because we are moving towards it, intentionally.
5. Now: We can focus on a plan to continue to move forward, towards that goal or target.

You can also stop at step #2 if you decide you're not going to do anything. *Thoughts do become things, if we allow them to evolve.*

One of my favorite mentors, Les Brown, hosted a workshop called the "Mindset Behind the Money." He is an awesome example of healthy mindset. It wasn't easy for him! Les was brought up in a very poor home in the projects. He was a twin, and was nicknamed the *Dumb Twin,* and was told he was retarded in school.

He had some pivotal mentors that helped him break through his initial mindset that was rather forced upon him, and he started allowing, and then going after his dreams one step at a time. He knew he needed a massive break to make his dream come true of being the most loved Inspirational Speaker in the world. But, he didn't wait, hoping for his break to happen. Les completely manifested it from start to finish!

He knew he needed to do something huge to catapult his speaking career. He needed a stage. A big one. He wanted to be on a show that was very popular back in its day: The Robert Schuller TV program. He called them, but the "gatekeepers" of the show kept him out. He wasn't famous (yet) or a published author. Most people would have stopped and given up right there, which is why most people in his field won't achieve what he has.

What did Les do? Oh man, I love this part! He would say to everyone that he met, "Hello I'm Les Brown, and I'm going to be on the Robert Schuller program!" They would typically respond by saying, "That's great! When?" And, Les would answer, "I don't know yet. Do YOU know Robert Schuller?" Usually they would respond, "No, I'm sorry I do not."

But, one day on a plane, things changed. The gentlemen sitting next to him (a nice captive audience by the way) responded to Les and said, "Yes, yes I do know him. In fact, I know someone who just gave the Robert Schuller show one million dollars in support!"

The bottom line? Les got on the show, multiple times. Les also got a large, lucrative speaking gig from his new friend he met on the plane. SCORE. Game Changer. Life Changer. And a Destiny Maker. *A destiny created by God, and moved forward by Les.*

Your mindset is like a garden.
What you plant there grows. What seeds are you planting? And are you pulling the weeds regularly? Are you watering the soil and fertilizing your precious seeds? Are you in good sunlight to raise the growth upward? And if you were telling truth right now: are you bearing fruit? How much? How good is it? *And, are you sharing your fruit with others?*

Fuel for your flame:
What do you currently do to feed your mindset?
Is there anything you need to implement to grow a healthy mindset, or anything you need to cut out of what you currently do or think about?

Chapter 11: Balance
by Sheli G

Fluidity, i.e. your healthy flow of doing and being, will cause your best results as well as your daily and life-long significance, as you find your purpose on this planet, and fulfill it. ~ Sheli G

Flow with fluidity as you move towards what needs to be done, intentionally prioritizing all of your precious, limited resources, as only you can do for you. ~ Sheli G

When I think of balance, I imagine a scale where each side hangs perfectly level with the other. HA! Okay sorry, but I've *never* been like this in my life. Have you? It's like the impossible dream! Yet we talk in our culture all the time about *balance*. What a dis-empowering thought for so many.

The Message
What is the idea of balance? Spending equal amounts of time on all things? Well, good luck achieving that. If you work full time, you already spend more hours there than at home or play. Does this mean that your work is more important? No, not necessarily. For many of us, humanitarian or spiritual things get fit in as much as possible, and they are often the *most* important things we do! Friends, vacations, exercising, organizing, self-improvement...most of us work all these things in as often as we can, and oftentimes it doesn't feel like we have enough time or energy. Is balance about how we feel? I sure hope not. Feelings alone are rarely a good reality check.

So just know, *balance isn't only about how you feel.*
To confuse this balance issue even more, let's talk about defining it. If you ask ten different people, you would get ten different answers. Or, you might get people using general descriptors like, "Balance is having all things in order in your life, with priorities

in place so you can be fulfilled." Okay….?

The vagueness of definitions like that can make others feel like; "WOW, how can I ever do that!? My life in order? Priorities all lined up (perfectly)? That whole *balance thing* must be for someone else, not me. I'm not that_____." fill in the blank here...organized, mature, grounded, spiritual, selfless, driven, etc.

I think of balancing my life as an ongoing process, where I'm continually assessing myself.
How am I doing? How am I stewarding my time right now, and is that working? 1. Where do I need to stop spending time and energy? 2. Where or what or who do I need to spend more time on or with? 3. What needs some "Hyper Focus" today, or this week, or month?

Life changes constantly. Our passions evolve. Our family and the people around us change. The economy churns out its crazy spins and twisters. Jobs, relationships and opportunities come and go.

So, is finding our own balance really more about adapting and re-aligning constantly to achieve whatever is the most important to us at that time? Maybe it's about stewarding the precious time and energy we have daily, weekly, monthly… to the best of our ability?

I believe that being healthy; body, mind and spirit, automatically helps you to ask yourself and then to prioritize your physical, emotional, financial and other resources naturally. When you are in tune inside and out, you will always be re-aligning and adjusting the sails of your life to do your highest and best. No one else can decide what balance is for you. If they try to, see the chapter on Boundaries again! *Only you, in a healthy state of mind, can do this for you.*

Balance then, I am suggesting, is more fluid and changing.
Certain core beliefs and our values will always take their highest
roles with each of us as we've defined them. Even so, the day to
day, and weekly or monthly tasks associated with those core
values will ebb and flow, according to what needs to be done.
What needs attention, what is urgent, what can wait, and
everything in between. Move with fluidity, as you focus on what
needs to be done. Intentionally prioritize all of your precious,
limited resources as only you can do for you.

Fuel for your flame:
How would you define balance, for you?
When you feel really out of balance, how do you correct that, or
how could you begin to correct that in your life?

Chapter 12: Health
by Terilee

Dear Body,
I apologize for being mean to you. Let's be friends from now on.
Love, Me. ~ Unknown

In general, where do you imagine the average person will fall on a scale of 1-10 regarding their physical or body health?
1 = Never exercise.
5 = Yo-yo diet and sometimes exercise.
10 = Always workout consistently.

How do you rate your overall Health on a scale of 1-10? _____

I reached out to a fitness expert, Brian Kelly, Founder of GlobalFitnessClub.com, for some answers. According to Brian, the average person falls between a 3-5 out of 10.

The Message
When I asked Brian, "Why are the ratings so low?" he shared, "Folks try to go it alone. It's far too easy to succumb to excuses when you rely solely on yourself. An accountability/workout partner does wonders."

Another reason is priorities. "Fitness is all too often placed way too far down the list of one's priorities. It comes down to developing a 'champion' mindset. This can be done easily with the proper guidance."

Rating analysis.
I will shamelessly confess my ratings have been low in the past because I was always the "last one picked." Our beliefs from our childhood can stick with us like Super Glue. I was one of the wimpy girls in school. I hated PE. I wasn't coordinated or real

strong physically. If we picked teams, I was ALWAYS the last one picked.

No one ever wants to be the last one picked. Standing there in line. Getting ready to play kickball. Waiting. Waiting some more. Feeling unwanted. Feeling untalented. Even your best friends don't want you on their team. Your classmates don't believe in your ability. And, deep down, you don't believe in yourself either.

When you grow up believing you are not good at something, it is amazing how that can play out over the course of your life. When you believe you are not athletic as a child, do you grow up to be an adult who exercises?

A Story of Inspiration.
My mom, Bobbie Tussing, was sick my entire life. She was diagnosed with Juvenile Diabetes in 1955 when she was only 13 years old.

How many diabetics do you know who still eat sweets? My mom had extreme fortitude when it came to sticking to her diet. She was 26 years old when I was born. My sister, LeAnn, came along two years later. Once she had us girls, she NEVER cheated on her diet. She had a strong conviction that she wanted to live as long as possible to be there for us. I cannot remember one time she cheated on her diet.

What's more, she struggled with other stomach issues, so if she found something to eat for breakfast that didn't upset her stomach, she would eat it for breakfast every single day. She would have eggs, toast, and oatmeal every single day. She ate lots of tuna over the years for lunch…every single day. She ate lots of baked turkey for supper (we called it *supper*) every single day.

I remember one year for her birthday, my sister and I made our entire family what Mom was going to have for dinner so we could eat together. Now I wish we hadn't just done that *one* year! On occasion, when I was younger, there were a few restaurants where she could find something she could eat. My grandparents (her parents) loved to take us out when they would visit. I am sure they enjoyed treating her to something she could enjoy since this didn't happen too often. As time passed and she had more stomach issues, she always packed her meals and would take them with her. This was all normal to us at the time.

Even living this diligently, her Diabetes eventually took its toll on her body. She passed away in 2000 at the age of 58.

I miss her so much, but I am grateful for the years I had with her and will always remember her sacrifice to not sneak a bite of chocolate cake here or there and enjoy the temporary pleasure because being there for me (and my entire family) was more important to her.

How many people do you know with Diabetes, high blood pressure, heart issues, or food allergies who still eat what they aren't supposed to from time-to-time? I know many people like this.

Truth be told, I'm one of those people.
When I eat gluten, I feel like I've been hit by a truck afterward and many times, I feel like I need to lay down and rest. Knowing this, there are still times, I will order a sandwich instead of a salad at lunch. I knowingly make the choice, and know I am accepting the consequences of not feeling good. I have been doing a much better job with this as I write this book, but I wouldn't be honest with you if I didn't admit if I'm out to eat and my entire party is enjoying some yummy pizza, I still struggle with the temptation.

The more I control what I eat and the more I exercise, the more I realize how good I feel, and the more I want to avoid it. It also helps to be reminded of my Mom's fortitude and the great love she showed for my entire family.

Get inspired.

When I grow up, I want to be like Maxine. I met Maxine the day I signed up for the program where I work out. As I was signing paperwork to join, I was secretly thinking, "I'm not *really* sure I want to be here." But then, out of the corner of my eye, I saw Maxine working out in beast mode, planking, and totally in shape. The owner noticed me checking her out and said, "That's Maxine, and she's 82 years old." Seriously? That is so cool! If I change my ways now and take good care of myself, I can be like Maxine? I'm in! What or who inspires you to better health? Find what inspires you and get to it!

It is an amazing thing to have finally embraced that I have only one body for this life. I need to take the best care of it possible now so I can enjoy more life later. *I deserve the best, and so does my body.*

Fuel for your flame:

Is it time for change? The first step to getting anywhere is deciding you're not willing to stay where you are. I don't want to stay where I am.

How about you? What change would you like to make? Strive for progress, not perfection.

What is one step you can take today to begin to make progress?

Chapter 13: Faith
by Terilee

*Let your faith be bigger than
your fear. ~ Unknown*

*...You're not yet taking God seriously," said Jesus. "The simple truth is
that if you had a mere kernel of **faith**, you would tell this mountain,
'Move!' and it would move. There is nothing you wouldn't be able to
tackle. ~ Matthew 17:20*

*When you are truly called to it, jump. Let God and your experience
build your beautiful wings on the way, as you learn how to fly.
~ Sheli G*

Faith is confidence or trust in a person or thing.

The Message
I love the little ones I teach at church. You never know what they
are going to say! There was a time when they asked me to read
them the story of the blind man over and over for several weeks
in a row. We can learn about faith from the blind man,
Bartimaeus. Bartimaeus was sitting by the road, and he could
hear lots of noise and people around him. "What is happening?"
he asked. "Jesus is coming," someone told him. He began calling
for Jesus. There was a big crowd, yet as Jesus was coming by, He
heard him. "What can I do for you? He asked the blind man. "I
know you can make me well," was his reply. Jesus said, "Your
faith has healed you." And then Bartimaeus could see.

Do you believe in miracles? Bartimaeus did. He had confidence
that he could be healed. There was no question in his mind. He
held absolute certainty in his heart. This is what faith is. I don't
know about you, but I want to live with extraordinary faith like
that in all areas of my life.

Faith in your dream.

What is your dream? Your big, audacious dream. Maybe it's for your business. Maybe it's your purpose or calling. Sometimes life is about risking everything for a dream no one can see but you. If you don't have faith in your dream, others won't follow you. You have to see it, smell it, taste it, and feel it 24/7. *Is your faith in your dream a Level 10 EVERY DAY so on the tough days it's enough to see you through?*

Faith in yourself.

Have you ever lost faith in your dream (even temporarily) because you really just lost faith in yourself? You didn't believe in yourself. Deep down, you didn't like yourself, and so you sabotaged your dream because you weren't ready for it. Loving yourself is a vital foundation to having faith in yourself. Knowing your gifts and being ready to exercise and use them at any given time will help you build faith in yourself, too.

How many times in business have you had to learn something new and then show up in confidence and share it with other people? Perhaps it's a new speech. Pitching a new program to some higher level clients than you have ever presented to before. Interviewing on live television. Helping a colleague resolve a conflict. The list could go on and on! Have you ever wanted to take a mentor with you and rely on them to do the job because you weren't sure you had faith in yourself? (You probably know what I'm talking about.) The only way to grow confidence and gain experience is to put yourself in charge and do that new thing. #youknowmorethanyouthinkyouknow

Faith in God.

If faith in God is important to you, like it is to me, it is the very basis on which (I try my best) to make all my decisions. As I travel on my journey, I am grateful for my experiences, especially my challenges, which cause my faith in God to grow. *He has been so good to me!*

Faith in action.

Faith without action is nothing. You will always feel fear about the things you need to do to accomplish your goals and dreams. Here's the deal: You will NEVER feel completely ready. The key is to take action amidst the fear and do what you need to anyway. Every time I have tried something new that scared me, afterward I am always so glad I did! *Do it afraid.*

Fuel for your flame:

How much faith do you have in your dream?

Or, if you have not narrowed in on one yet, do you have faith that you will?

Deep down, truthfully, how much faith do you have in yourself? Scale of 1-10, 1 being no faith, 10 being complete faith.

Chapter 14: Justice
by Sheli G

To realize the fullness of your calling and dreams, you must truly align yourself with a greater vision of the world, and your part, however big or small, in making it come to fruition. That is to be just. ~ Sheli G

This is a MASSIVE topic for this time, in our culture, and in the world.

Justice (as defined by dictionary.reference.com):
The quality of being just; righteousness, equitableness, or moral rightness: To uphold the justice of a cause.

The Message
I love the Millennials (who don't like to be called that, by the way) – the young adults who have really brought this subject to a burning point in American culture today.

How each one defines Justice may be unique.
Individualization is actually part of justice.

But, for *The Ignited Entrepreneur*, what is justice? How does it relate to your brand? How does it relate to the problem that your product or service speaks to or solves? How do you as a leader or entrepreneur model justice in your company, circles, and at home?

What is a brand or product if it doesn't make an individual, a group, or the world better? So, what does your platform offer? Not only is that a valid question, I think, for the authentic, modern leader, but it's also trending *for a reason*.

When a product or service can help make the planet a more just place for someone or everyone, by either being more green/eco-friendly, serving equality, bettering our health, offering freedom, evolving education, giving opportunity, bettering communication, standing up to evil, promoting health and wellness, offering enlightenment, and so on, it has a far better chance of surviving its competition.

We have a collective understanding (a general awareness spanning the globe) that we are all connected. We know that everything is connected. This understanding is translating now into business vision and strategy as well, as it should.

Products like Apple have made it possible for people in the most remote parts of the planet to connect with others, become more educated, and attain valuable information that can even support their very survival. Like medical information found online in the jungle, when there is no hospital or even a clinic nearby.

Tom's shoes are not only fashionable, (especially my pink glittery ones, don't judge me) but they also send a pair of Tom's shoes to a person in need when you buy them. No wonder they have totally rocked their brand.

Terilee and I have a friend who is the CEO of a company called Cherished High Desert. Cherished provides therapist-led support groups for women, whether they are in or out of the industry. Cherished is also a social enterprise and residential program. **www.cherishedhighdesert.com**

At IgniteSouls.com I feel a responsibility, which I call "a beautiful burden", to use the "stage" if you will, both in live and online events, to promote justice, in the way I define it. I feel passionate to model this to others. We celebrate all peoples, and the unique gifts we all bring. We want to not only disrupt, but shatter any of the walls that divide us. We want to compassionately collaborate, not compete.

I have seen both phenomenal leaders, and pathetic ones. A "leader" I worked for at a local Mexican Restaurant sexually harassed me and others, stole from the company, and sold drugs at work. That was not good modeling of justice. It was a show of misguided and misused power. We have far too much of that today in government, companies, even in non-profits in the name of *justice*.

In my "past life" I worked at a huge mortgage company. The larger they grew, the more our paychecks were cut back. It was really odd, and did not necessarily promote that sense of justice amongst their tribe. But, it helped me to leave and start my next company, which was the upside! There are no accidents after all. Good news!

I remember one real giver. He was a mentor in my life in ways he probably still doesn't realize. I need to give him a call, which reminds me! His name was Steve. Steve mentored me in business dealings, and also in life from a spiritual perspective. He is a very successful man in all aspects of life.

One day, I called him after I had shut the doors of my first business (yes, I am a serial entrepreneur). A lot had transpired, and in order to leave that business behind, I took with me thousands of dollars in debt that I was making payments on. It was very tough. I had a bad month, and I wasn't able to make ends meet, and I had one bill creditor call the loan "due in full" immediately. It was about a five hundred dollar balance, which in that moment, seemed like a bunch.

He had called me that day just to check in, and I was emotional and frustrated. Next thing I knew, he showed up at my work, called me to come outside, and handed me a check to cover that bill. I was so blown away. Yes, he certainly got me out of a bind at that moment. But, much bigger than that, he was always doing selfless things to help others; things no one else would ever know about. For him, it was a sense of justice, or doing what was right. *For him, it was right to do his part and to give back, and help someone in need.*

Doing the right thing, at the right time, for the right reasons. Justice. Helping those who cannot help themselves.
The Bible in Proverbs 3:27 says "Never walk away from someone who needs help, your hands are God's hands for that person." *That's powerful.*

In high school, I often found myself defending those whom others bullied and picked on. I had a friend Mike who had Dyslexia, Scoliosis, and other challenges. He had surgery at one point that allowed him to grow six inches in height! Missing so much school was tough on him. But, Mike kept the best attitude. He was beyond courageous. As I look back even now, it was astonishing the character he had, and the strength. I don't even remember specifically what the kids would do and say, I just remember it was wrong, it was bullying, and I naturally defended him. *It was undoubtedly the right thing to do.*

Some years later, Mike contacted me and said that he had gone to college and graduated, and now had a great bank job. He said that he was brave enough to go to college, and graduate, partly due to me and a few others having faith in him and defending him all those years ago. I was blown away. It was in my mind, a small, natural thing from an innate place, and a cultural sense of justice and respect (cultural, in the way I was raised and our beliefs).

To stand for justice, we don't have to run for office. We don't have to be a cop, a priest, a paramedic, or an attorney. We don't have to join the Peace Corp. I mean we can...but there are also a billion tiny and large things we can do to promote justice in any given moment. We can do these things no matter what family we come from, no matter how much money is in our bank account, no matter what profession or job we hold, and no matter what position or role we play.

We can first teach and model justice to our own families in every word and deed – no matter if we're out in public or behind closed doors where no one sees. We can pick up trash on the street. We can yield to someone in traffic. We can give what we can to those in need: food, money, resources, time, training, a smile, perspective, and hope. We can serve on boards that need our expertise. We can post on our socials, blogs, emails, and web sites content that is positive, true, valuable, healing, informative, and serving. We can diligently grow our leadership and communication skills, so that as leaders and entrepreneurs, we not only scale our businesses, we can mentor others to be amazing leaders and to give back too. It's not just an opportunity in my opinion. It's a responsibility. *It's a beautiful burden of The Ignited Entrepreneur, if you are willing.*

Fuel for your flame:
How do you use your abilities to promote justice in the world?
What is an injustice that you are frustrated with? Can you help?

Chapter 15: Giving
by Sheli G

To handle yourself, use your head;
to handle others, use your heart.
~ Eleanor Roosevelt

I believe just like a coach or a speaker should not live any differently than what they teach, preach, or speak about. An individual or company should always be congruent with what they say their message is... otherwise, I question their message. ~ Sheli G

Giving has always been in style. It's trending even more today. Books like The Go Giver and many similar to it have flooded the markets and mindsets of individuals and companies. And there are master networkers like my friends Ivan and Beth Misner, Co-Owners of BNI. The philosophy of their organization is built upon the idea of Givers Gain®: By giving business to others, you will get business in return. This is predicated on the age-old idea of *what goes around, comes around.*

They have successfully set a pretty high standard for giving selflessly in the professional zone and beyond. What I appreciate about Ivan and Beth is that they LIVE it in their lives, even when nobody is watching them.

The Message
Call it karma, the Golden Rule, or just the right thing to do...it seems to be catching on. Or, is it?

The wealthy including business people, celebrities, athletes and the occasional socialite, also either legitimately give financially from their heart and a sense of "paying it forward," or sometimes they give for a much needed tax break, or even simply from a place of gaining exposure or good press. Giving can show up as simply part of the overall marketing strategy of a company or individual.

But real giving is so much more. In fact, if you think about it, unless you're really struggling, most healthy people _want_ to give.

They want to give of whatever they have, beyond just money. Giving of time, energy, mentoring, passing down things that they are not using anymore, the sharing of ideas or wisdom. Being a mentor, serving on a board, being in a mastermind, volunteering. There are so many examples.

There is giving when it's accounted for, like at a live event. At IgniteSouls.com we create events where we can give back. Giving is seen from the stage at live conferences and events. Although, I believe that some of the best giving is done in private. It's the coaching skype that no one sees. The giving of funds anonymously. The mentoring. It's praying for someone. It's the emergency calls. The conflict resolution. The marriages that need hope. It's the food, clothing or other needs that are met when no one knows, and when nobody is looking. And those precious moments, given in private, with no expectation of anything in return..._they may be the best._

So I guess there is a return.
It fills up my heart and spirit. Then I want to do more. It's beautiful how it works. _Have you experienced that?_

I believe just like a coach or a speaker should not live any different than what they teach, preach, or speak about. An individual or company should always be congruent with what they say their message is, otherwise, _I question their message._

People tell themselves stories about themselves.
They sell themselves first, and then they sell it to others. But, if who you are, what you think about when you are alone, what you do when you are tempted (and no one will ever know but you and God), what you watch on TV or your computer or smart device, what you say and do, what you eat and practice...if they

are not all congruent with who you SAY you are and what you CLAIM your message is, then either 1. it's not really your message and belief, or 2. you need to evaluate how to get in alignment with your message and beliefs. I know from working with people for more than 20 years, that they want to give and serve others…when they are healthy.

Fuel Your Flame
Are you giving, even when nobody is looking, and you don't stand to measure the gain?
Why do you give? Or if you don't give enough, why not?

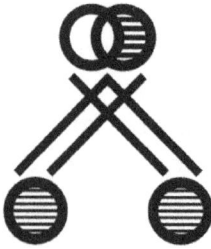

Chapter 16: Kids
by Sheli G

Your hardest job ever will be parenting, if you do it with all your heart. ~ Sheli G

Don't give up all of your quality time with your kids today, for a dream you hope will manifest into fortunes and or fame tomorrow, or you may lose the right to both opportunities. ~ Sheli G

Remember, you can't take your businesses, inventions or money to heaven. But, if you do a good job, hopefully someday your kids will meet you there. ~ Sheli G

There is a Christmas musical where the main song is: "A Baby Changes Everything" and yes, I concur. I'm sure all parents would agree.

The Message
Balancing children as an entrepreneur is tough and achievable. Again, balance is defined by you! (See the balance chapter)

At this particular moment, I am so tired from wrangling my children all day that I cannot even take this chapter on! See you tomorrow when I hope and pray, God has rejuvenated my cells and spirit!

Okay good news…I'm back and rejuved!

Yesterday, I was coaching an executive client, and she brought up that she feels women are wondering inside how it's possible to have it all (*all* being defined as *everything that we want*). Family. Career. Faith. Charitable pursuits. Friends. Solitude. Free time. Health. Wealth…or whatever is on your list.

I think men are asking this, too. With more women working

today, and even women who don't work, being busier than ever with the PTA, charitable events, kids sports, and volunteering, men are expected more than ever to share in the day to day household tasks and childcare duties.

Only you know your priorities, goals, and responsibilities.
No one can tell you how your day, career or family should look. But, I will share a few things that I have learned over time that have helped me as the serial entrepreneur, wife, mother, humanitarian, volunteer, daughter, musician, sister, etc.

Prioritize.
Easier said than done. But, daily and sometimes even hourly, I revisit what needs to be done, in the order of importance or urgency. Sometimes there is a critical business meeting that will happen, short of an emergency! No matter what obstacle life throws up on me.

That's a priority. And, when the school calls because my child is sick – BAM! Instant priority. All else is moved back. When my Women Ignite Conference draws near, what I call "Hyper Focus" comes into play. Laundry backs up a bit, emails get an auto response that I'm in full conference mode, and I'll get back to them ASAP (but later than usual). I reduce my consulting and coaching to urgent or high priority clients only. *After a conference or big event, it's time to rest, hunker down with my kids in our pajamas uninterrupted, with hot cocoa and love on each other.*

How do you set your priorities?
Time Blocking.
Prioritizing leads me to time block. I find the important things need blocks of secured time. Work appointments of course, we know about showing up to schedule meetings, but time blocking applies to all tasks needed to get accomplished! That includes study time, paperwork filing, research, phone calls, doing email, and the list goes on.

Our personal lives demand blocks of time also. Blocks of time with family, doing chores, sleeping, entertainment, hobbies, friends, health. Keeping those blocked out times is so important, like they are an appointment with the President! Or like it's an appointment with the person you'd love to have a meeting with: Steve Jobs, Oprah Winfrey, Richard Branson, Carrie Underwood or whomever lights your fire! (Terilee and Sheli G!) You deserve to keep that appointment, that sacred blocked out time, for the purpose of why you needed it by priority and urgency. Don't break your appointment with you, unless it's an emergency. Period. *Keep your word to yourself.*

Most of us value honesty and integrity in business and friendships, but if you don't keep your word to yourself, you have something to look at that I suggest needs adjustment. If you don't respect your time, goals and priorities, don't expect others too. *We train others how to respect and treat us.*

Forgiving.
Forgive your kids, they will frustrate the crap out of you at times, if you are truly engaged. Forgive your spouse or significant other, they too will at times, make you want to poke your eyes out. Forgive others, who oftentimes seem to act or speak to you like they know what's best for your kids, even when you have not asked for their superior input. Forgive the world for the evil that lurks, that will try to take your kids if you are not really prioritizing them. Forgive it, but don't let it win. And mostly, forgive yourself. You will screw some stuff up. You will learn too. You will have epic fails (sometimes in front of an audience). You will do some things amazingly right and good too. You will say the wrong thing, miss something important or overstep your reach...and you will apologize and model to your kids that although we screw it up, we can own our mistakes, learn lessons, and then move on. Forgive often, freely and without cause, as you also would like to receive that forgiveness cup.

Don't project.
Your kiddos are unique. No, really. *They, like you, are one of a kind.*
They are not you. I know sometimes they look like us, act like us,
even talk like us! But they are their own person with strengths
that are as different from ours, and they may seem similar to us
in other ways. They are growing up with different parents than
we did! *They are in a culture that is radically different than when we
were kids.*

Although we may share some family bonds, or DNA coding,
never forget that they are not you. Don't try to push your
agendas, goals, perceptions, judgements, schedules, beliefs, or
expectations on them. Educate them of course in the things that
you believe matter. But, they will still some day need the space to
research those things, experience their own transformational
moments of breakthrough, and make their own choices as an
adult. *They will screw it up, too, sometimes.*

Kids don't exist to fulfill a plan we set up for them.
They don't exist to make us happy or proud. They, like you,
came to this planet with a divine purpose, that only they can
fulfill, if they so choose. Their purpose on this planet may look
wholly different than you thought it would, but doesn't your
purpose look somewhat different than you assumed it would,
too? Support your cherubs in being the best that they are born to
be.

*It's their journey. Be grateful you were chosen to be some of the wind
beneath their precious wings.*

Fuel for your flame:
What do my kids or other children in my life deserve from me
this week?
Are my priorities in order for my family? If not, what needs to be
re-aligned?

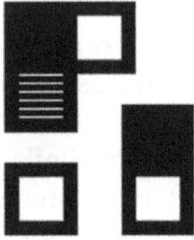

Chapter 17: Organization
by Sheli G

This word either makes you feel fabulous about yourself, question yourself, or bow your head in shame.

I personally have felt all of these stages of organization, or lack thereof, at different times in my life. Your level of ability and commitment in this area is usually something that is partly learned in childhood, it's partly cultural, and also your personality and strengths factor in.

Your level of organization can greatly impact things like your meetings, your efficiency, your errors, your self-esteem, your preparedness and ultimately your results and reputation.

If you are a master organizer, then you probably teach classes on this and have little growth needed. But, if you struggle in some areas of organization, there are a lot of resources to help in many areas of business and your personal life.

How organized you are in your personal life certainly impacts your business, from your self-esteem to actual challenges that distract you professionally. The same is true of work; if you're chaotic at work, with administration, HR, your technology, employee communication, taxes, and so on...that stress can transfer straight into your personal life.

There are books and classes dedicated to this topic, so I won't make it a focal point in ours. I am not an "expert" in this area. However, I will share a few practical things from my experience that I think are helpful.

One powerful organizational tool has been my iPad mini. It may depend on the type of industry you are in, but being able to carry around a small computer, everywhere, lets me be prepared no matter what. There is never *dead time* when my appointment is late, or cancels, or I arrive somewhere early, or find a natural break in my day, or a nice working moment comes...I have almost everything I need for work.

When I get "tiny breaks" I tend to:
- Check emails, and answer the important ones
- Check text messages and answer
- Create business content, to-do lists and pictures with text
- Post to my many business social pages and platforms
- If I have WIFI, I can use my iPad to text, just like it's my cell

For longer time opportunities I can:
- Work on projects that are stored in my notepad. These save automatically, and then I have them with me everywhere.
- I can write in my book :)
- I can write a blog or article
- I can take a quick "on location" video
- Go into my Google Drive and create, add to or share documents
- Use my cell and return longer calls

One of my favorite organizational components about my iPad is that instead of having various notepads, journals, and notebooks, I have my slim iPad that fits great in any purse. It stores notes or lists from any class, meeting, seminar, or idea, they save automatically, and I can email them to myself or anyone else easily with WIFI. Save paper! There is less organizing to do later, because it's all in there by name and date, and I can search for notes anytime and anyplace. It also syncs to my iPhone, so I can look up those lists or notes there, too.

More organizational tools: **Apps.** Most of us use them. It's a matter of what you need based on your business, your strengths and your challenges. Stellar GPS apps work really well for me! I am admittedly directionally impaired – legitimately. Now, I never take a wrong turn. Also, receipt apps that take pics of receipts and file them immediately prepare you along the way for your CPA. Mileage and expense apps, voice recording, voice dictation (good for writing on the road), and the list never ends. A new app was created in this very second, I am sure of it!

Speaking of numbers and tracking, unless you are awesome at taxes, let someone else do that! There are brilliant CPA's, attorneys, financial planners, virtual assistants, and web designers...so let the masters do their jobs. It will take way less time, they will do a way better job than you, and you can focus on what *you* are brilliant at.

I am a big fan of organizers as a profession! If they are good, they have amazing ideas and resources that you would never think of, based on their gifts and experience. After they've worked with every kind of client, every type of room, and hundreds of organizational tools and designs, they can objectively look at any mess and have a vision for not only aesthetically what could be, but from an uber-organized and efficient functionality standpoint. Once again, there are masters at this. Don't dabble in it and stay in frustrated scenarios.

These days, our office can travel with us. With laptops, iPads, smart phones, and more, we can essentially be ready all the time for almost any need. Take it all with you, everywhere in town you go. You never know how the day will flow, so be prepared.

Paper Planners.
Yep. Here's a throwback idea: I have switched back to a paper planner. Not just any planner, it's one customized to me. It has daily, monthly, and yearly sections for goals, to-do lists, and contacts. It also has a space for my fave, *Mind Mapping*, which helps me get my ga-billion ideations out onto paper so my brain can relax and focus on one at a time. Google "Mind Mapping" if

you have not tried it. It's cool!

They have mileage trackers too, for those who just want a notebook for that in their car at all times. As a speaker/facilitator, I like to look out months ahead. I need to. For me, it's better than my smartphone. You have to do what works for you. With a lot of organizational stuff, it's not right or wrong. It's just how you work, think, and operate and what tools, tricks, apps, or systems will best support you. And, FYI, your team members, if you have them, will need to do some individual systems to support themselves, too. Generally speaking, an Engineer versus an Artist will schedule and organize their day very differently.

Those are just a few of the simple things that have helped me. It's time to assess where you need some support.

Fuel for your flame:
On a scale of 1-10, 1 being not at all and 10 being perfectly organized professionally, where are you?
What one thing could you do or act on this week that could help you in a professional area that needs more organizational help?

Chapter 18: Laughter
by Terilee

Always find a reason to laugh. It may not add years to your life, but it will add life to your years. ~ Unknown

People may forget what you said, they may forget what you did, but they will never forget how you made them feel. ~ Maya Angelou

We've all heard the phrase "laughter is the best medicine." But have you heard that "laughter is the fireworks of the soul?" Think about the last time you saw fireworks. How did seeing the fireworks make you feel? Did you feel awakened? Enlightened? Provoked? Stirred? Thrilled?

Truth be told, in the stormy times it can be hard to laugh. I love being silly, saying funny things, and I think laughing is awesome. But, when you are depressed, struggling to care for a critically ill family member, are out of work, don't believe in yourself, or when you are hanging onto the past, it can be really difficult to find anything to laugh about.

If you have been finding it hard to laugh lately, you are in the right place. Sheli G and I are here to help you. This is all the more reason to work on your stuff and let it go. There are mental health benefits to laughter to help you feel better: It adds joy and zest to life, eases anxiety and fear, relieves stress, boosts your immune system, improves mood, and can enhance resilience.

The Message
Being able to laugh with others is a gift. My girlfriend and I get into some major texting conversations on a daily basis. Now you must understand that Nancy Burroughs is a respected speaker and relationship expert. This brings a certain amount of

seriousness. But, sometimes Terry and I are sitting on the couch watching TV and she and I will be texting. She will send over a hilarious comment, and suddenly I'm falling off the couch laughing. Literally. Terry will help me back up on the couch and knowingly ask, "What did she say now?" and I let him in on the joke. I LOVE laughing like that.

A story about snorting:
Snorting is an uncontrollable burst of laughter that explodes out your nose. Immediately following most good snorts comes more giggling and laughter. It's awesome and contagious.

(Hi. This is Sheli G, and I *adore* this explanation of snorting.
Okay, as you were.)

If you know Sheli G, you know she snorts *occasionally* (or a lot) when she laughs. I love it when she snorts. In fact, I snort on occasion, too, but I really only snort when I'm with her.

Sheli G and I traveled to Ecuador together in January, 2015. Our Translator, Trevor Allen, who traveled everywhere with us snorts, too. I have not laughed as hard in years as I did during those seven days in South America with Sheli and Trevor, and we worked almost the entire time! It felt SO good to laugh like that.

There are social benefits to laughter that you may not be aware of. It strengthens relationships, attracts others to us, enhances teamwork, helps defuse conflict, and promotes group bonding. Trust me, Sheli, Trevor, and I are bonded now!

I work hard. By the end of each day, I'm tired. I also tend to overbook my schedule. That's a whole separate chapter, I'm sure. There's nothing like a good laugh to refresh my spirit in the middle of my work. Did you know there are physical health benefits to laughter? It boosts immunity, lowers stress hormones, decreases pain, relaxes your muscles, and can prevent heart disease. *I don't know about you, but I'll take all the physical health benefits I can get!*

Last but not least, it's important to be able to laugh at yourself. Nobody likes to be laughed at. It doesn't feel good when people make fun of you, but it is healthy to be able to laugh at yourself. Don't take yourself so seriously! These days I always laugh about my memory or what's left of it.

It's vital to be self-confident and believe in yourself so when someone says something to you about some quirky thing you did, you can let it bounce right off you and laugh right with them. *Love yourself enough to be able to laugh at yourself when things happen.*

This is Sheli G reporting in on Terilee's Laughter chapter. My husband, Steve, and I were in Los Angeles for a fabulous speaker's boot camp with International Super Speaker and Speaker's Coach, Les Brown.

I noticed that when I listen to Les, live at any event or even on YouTube, he is a masterful storyteller. He is also hysterical! And, even when what he says is not hilarious in content alone, he is laughing...hard...at himself! In fact, the last time I called him, his personal voice mail message/greeting ends with him just *laughing*! It's one of my FAVE things about Les. As an avid people watcher (who is with me here?), I notice the whole room loves it. You cannot help yourself. You just fall in love with this man. He makes you feel good. He makes you relax. He makes you laugh your face off. His classes, trainings and keynotes are awesome, too, but they are more like the frosting. I already get my value times a hundred just by the way *I feel* when I am with Les.

One time, I was sitting there, listening to him laugh, and I had a *significant* breakthrough. I love those.

I realized that I did not laugh very much when I was speaking on stage.
I would especially hold it back on a microphone. I did not know I was, but I did it subconsciously. I may have done that because I had a bit of a "loud laugher" complex, feeling like my laugh is too obnoxious, and for heaven's sake – I do SNORT. By the way, when you snort into a mic, you have to pause, because everyone usually laughs, and is totally distracted, and thinks you are drunk. #AmplifiedSnorting #Truth

It was time for me as a speaker to unlock more of myself. Authenticity is a BIG deal for me. Be who you are, *the same person*, at home, at work, on a stage or wherever. Laughing and snorting are part of the package that is Sheli G. It is part of who I am, and I have come to know that it is part of why people love me or enjoy hanging out with me. Since that breakthrough moment of learning more about myself, I have unlocked the whole Sheli-ness to show up on the stage or room: speaking passionately, teaching, inspiring, coaching, and laugh-snorting. It's awesome. I am having (way) more fun, and so are my audiences. #LaughSnort

Fuel for your flame:
Do I create opportunities for laughter in my life?
How can I bring more laughter to my world, and to those around me?

The Ignited Entrepreneur
Experiences It All

You will find yourself on all sides of rationality and the emotionality of The Ignited Entrepreneur, especially as a startup or if you take great risk at some point on your journey. There is dark, there is light, and there is breakthrough. ~Sheli G

Chapter 19: Calling
by Sheli G

I am the only one, but I am one. I cannot do everything, but I can do what I am called to do. I can do the purpose or calling on my life, and if I don't know what that is yet, then that can be my purpose: to discover my calling. I can make a difference one day, one project, one person or one movement at a time... let us begin! ~ Sheli G

What is your calling? Your purpose? There is a reason(s) you were created.

Do you know what calling is? Do you know that you have one? I believe you do. I've worked with people for 20 years now as a Life Mastery Coach. I've learned that healthy people all have some things in common:

- We all want to love and be loved.
- We all want to have our voice matter.
- We all feel at times like no one understands us (or like we are weird).
- We all want to be in service to mankind in some way.

- We all want to be significant, and we hope to leave a legacy.

The Message

These commonalities transcend gender, race, religion, geography and experience. They are just part of our DNA. I personally believe God made us this way, and gives us choice in how we go about attaining it. But, I believe at my core that we were all born and made with a purpose. Somehow, someway, we are all called to serve humanity. To find out what we can do, and to leave each soul better than we found them. This can look very different from person to person, as we travel each of our unique paths in life.

Our genetics, our upbringing, our individual strengths, our capabilities, and our collaboration with others all come together to lead us to the calling on our lives. Some know it from a young age. *Some search for that path for years before finding it.*

I believe some are in resistance to their calling.
Some people struggle with feeling not good enough. Or they are afraid to hope that there is a unique calling on their life, because they are worried that they may never know what that is. Some worry that they may fail at fulfilling their purpose. Or some shrink back, as they feel the responsibility of doing their part. In a world with so many massive needs, one can easily feel overwhelmed, especially if you don't realize that we are all in this together! You cannot save the whole world. (I know, I tried) *But you can do the things you are called to do.*

Good news: You don't have to have all the answers!
 Just bring the answers you **do** have, to those you **are** called to speak into, personally or professionally. You don't have to be perfect! You cannot lead people down a path you are not experienced or educated in, but you can lead people up to the place of your own expertise.

Just come as you are, accept the challenge that is calling to you, and do your audacious best, always. Learn as much as possible, in humility, as you go. *Then, lay your head on your pillow at night in peace, knowing you did all you could. That's a phenomenal feeling!*

We don't get anywhere in life that is remarkable and significant alone.

We don't get anywhere remarkable and significant in life, alone. Sometimes people will hurt you. They may let you down. I've heard thousands of stories in my work to prove it – really tough stories. But, we heal with others, too! We heal in community. Miracles happen in community. Healthy families, safe friends, coaches, mentors, counselors, books, and collaborating help us survive, be better, and scale.

I love the Spanish word for brainstorming (illuvia de ideas), because it means *to rain down ideas*. The best way to rain down ideas like a passionate, cleansing, ideating storm is in community.

Fuel for your flame:

Do you know what your calling, mission or purpose is?

If you do not know what your purpose is yet, what are the things you are the MOST passionate about? What do you soapbox about, cry over, get fired up about, desire to help in some way?

Chapter 20: Risk
by Sheli G

If you are not willing to risk the unusual, you will have to settle for the ordinary. ~Jim Rohn

I have known talented people who procrastinate indefinitely rather than risk failure. Lost opportunities cause erosion of confidence, and the downward spiral begins. ~Charles Stanley

The more you epic-risk, the more you epic-fail. Good news! The more you epic-risk, the more you EPIC-SUCCEED. ~Sheli G

Are you willing to take courageous, uncommon risks?
Let's go back in time. We are born onto the planet as naturally courageous kids. When you think about a little kid, what do you think of? Sometimes, they are just crazy, right? They're out on the playground, and they're out of their minds! They don't even know what they don't yet know, so they are just running and jumping without a thought or plan.

The adults (hopefully) grab them before they run out in front of a car. They will go right up to strangers, because they don't know the danger. And, of course, that's why we are there. Hopefully we all model to them some common sense, and provide them protection.

The Message
There is a beauty in childlike risk. By high school, people often begin to shut down. We begin to stop trusting, not only other people, circumstances and opportunities, *but we stop trusting ourselves.* We have reached out in the past and have been hurt. We have tried things and gotten damaged from them, or we did not receive the results that we expected. *People often stop risking out of fear.*

It's hard to reconcile the things that happen to us, that are out of our control.

People get abused in so many different forms. Bullying happens. We see teachers or authority figures that disappointed us greatly in their leadership. Maybe we are (or feel) lied to. Maybe we're physically hurt, verbally hurt, spiritually hurt, or otherwise. All we have to do is turn on the news and watch what's going on in our schools today, what's going on online, and even watch what's going on in our government, in our educational systems, in some corporations, and so on.

We so often go for "quick fixing" instead of problem solving in our culture.
It's the way we're raised up, trained, and what we see. It's what we see in movies. It's what we hear in much of our music, and it is what we see a lot of even in our authority figures. *I think we are falling tragically short of good role modeling from the top down in our country.*

Even many churches, who mean well, are a bit of a mess! It's why the young adults are exiting at a rapid rate. They are often too focused on programs, judgement and dressing up, *over meeting people where they are at, and loving on them without expectations.*

For clarity, I am not saying leave the church, or political office, or the school system. I believe the opposite.

Responsible citizens GET involved.
Be the change. Vote. Stay in it. Be the evolution you want to see. *We are leaders.* Don't quit...lead. Stand up for our educational system to empower our kids. Help change our Government back to being by and *for* the people again. And, get involved with your church or charity and be on the board and support with your voice and giftings. *These structures need us, and they desperately need bold, systemic change.*
#SermonOver #You'reWelcome

Sometimes we stop taking healthy risks.
We stop taking the kind of risks that we were born to take, the kind of risks that we came to the planet to take. There's literally millions of ways to do that. From the person that grows an organic garden that's free of pesticides and toxins, to the honorable educator, to the politician who's a truth-speaker, a love leader who has true character and an agenda to serve people, to the composer of music, to the author, entrepreneur, and to the missionary living a life of service to reach the unreached.

We all have something we're here to do.
And if you don't know what that is, I want to encourage you to find it, *but it's going to take risk.* Too often, people stuff their dreams and their visions. They quiet their voice. They sell out, and settle.

If we are not careful, we start to tell ourselves stories about ourselves about why we can't do it, why we shouldn't do it, why no one would listen to us, or why the risk is too great. When we take risks, we're going to "fail" IF failure means you don't get the result that you hoped for.

The more you epic-risk, the more you epic-fail. Good news! The more you epic-risk, the more you EPIC-SUCCEED. #BoomBaby

There is a lot of opposition around us and in us.
How many of us have been told in our childhood or in adulthood anything like this:

Don't do that, you will get hurt!
Are you crazy?
That was stupid.
That will teach you.
Don't be an idiot!
THAT is impossible.
It will never happen.

Think! Think!

You think you're going to monetize that?

You're a jerk.

You will never figure it out, will you?

You're just not very smart.

You're not as good as your sister, parents, team members, the national average.

This just isn't your thing.

You don't have what it takes.

Fill in what you heard here _____.

Don't believe it.

Everyone seems to be a self-appointed expert. And sometimes, the enemy within is the greatest obstacle. What is your self-talk? You know, that voice in your head that says mean, untruthful things to you. You need healthy, positive inner-talk going on, a ton, if you are going to achieve great things! If you don't like you, how can others? If you don't give yourself positive support to do all that you need to do day in and out, who will? *You are the one who is with you all the time, by the way!*

Here are a few ideas for working on that negative inner dialogue. I like to call that negative voice **"The Pig."** We can train the pig, but it never totally goes away. However, managing that negative talk when you notice it is powerful.

Ways to tame your pig:
1. <u>Notice what your inner dialogue is saying</u>. Write it down if needed for one week to see an objective amount of data. You can also record what times of the day, so that you might see a trend. For example: Mornings are tough, or late at night when I am tired.
2. <u>Replace it.</u> Find healthy, positive supportive talk, words, mantras that fit you, and are encouraging and uplifting to counteract the Pig. Ex: "I am feeling great today! I am ready to go! I know I can do this! I love my calling. I appreciate those around me. I will avoid toxic stimulus. I

will learn something new today. I will get closer to my goal. I am enough." And so on.

3. <u>Write some Positive ones down</u>. Write sticky notes for your bathroom mirror, rearview mirror, or computer. Wherever you will see them often. Put some on your vision board. Tell your friends and spouse so they can also lift you up.

4. <u>Change your passwords.</u> The bad news is, we all have 19,004 passwords. The good news is, the ones you use the most can be incredible positive mantra opportunities. It's an easy way to constantly realign your mindset. Ex: ICanDoIt1972, Hope2015, Newenergy89, PurposeRules01, and so on.

5. <u>Surround yourself with positive people.</u> As a leader, you need to be filled up, IGNITED, and re-energized to keep pouring into the lives of others.

6. <u>Start your morning with positive music, scriptures, affirmation downloads, videos, and books.</u> Be very careful what you put into your mind. It remembers. *Feed it well.*

Be willing to take bold action.
To take bold action, we deserve to stay positive. Yes, we will screw it up sometimes, or things will often go differently than we expected. But, miracles happen in an instant. We have an idea, a vision...and it takes wings when we allow it to! We meet someone, professionally or personally, that changes the land-scape of our business or life, forever. But, only if we risk. Only if we try. *Only if we get off the bench, and leave it all on the floor.*

Every time we act, we are automatically increasing our odds of success.
I am not really a baseball gal, *but* I found it really interesting that most of the baseball legends who are in the top 10 of the all-time baseball HOME RUN record kings, are in the same top 10 that were also the STRIKEOUT record kings. Take a chance. Lose some. #WINSome

Failure is only failure if you don't learn from it.
If I'm looking for who can lead a team well, the best leaders have had a lot of failures and successes. They have tasted success, and they know what it's like to lead a charge and have it go awesome. They also know what it's like to have the challenges and obstacles. That is why they are so skilled and experienced at navigating those waves, and encouraging others that *we can get through this, we can do this, we can find a way.*

We need phenomenal people in our lives that support us through great risks.
Family, friends, mentors or associates. We each have our own customized support system. If you don't have a really positive support system, it's going to be something that you need to have in order to get to the amazing places that your vision wants to take you, and your soul wants to take you.

Leaders find themselves in a sea of followers.
It makes sense, because leaders seem strong, confident, and clear, and so they will attract people that want to be led. They will attract those that need direction and support. *That's natural.*

The challenge for a leader is that if they're not paying attention, can end up *only* surrounded by all these people that need support and need direction. Leaders also need people to follow. Leaders need leaders. We need to find the mentors and advisors that can speak into our lives as well. Those who have gone before us and had some successes, challenges, and who are willing to share and bestow the wisdom from those experiences with us.

So what else does it take to take great risks?
Health. The healthier we are in all the different ways we need to be healthy, the more resilient you're going to be. Taking risk requires a lot of energy, effort, commitment, and consistency. And when I say energy, I mean physical energy, emotional energy, spiritual energy, financial energy; it takes energy in every way.

The healthier you are physically, the more stamina your body's going to have, the less days you're going to be sick, fatigued, depressed, or down and out. Treat your body as a temple, so that food becomes fuel. What grade of fuel are you eating? Fresh, organic, healthy foods, vegetables, fruits, and drinking a lot of purified water?

You are only a finely-tuned machine if you're finely-tuning your machine. It's the same thing with your mind.
Mind. What are you putting into your mind? Your mind is one of the most incredible, complicated organisms on the planet. It's so expansive in what it can do that we will never know all its potential. But, what are you downloading into your mind? What are you reading about? Is it valuable, is it good, is it propelling you forward, is it propelling the planet forward? Or, is it trash; is it negative, is it dark? What value are you creating? What value are you creating in what you watch on TV, on the internet, your computer, your phone, your iPad? What images are you looking at? What texts are you looking it? Is it valuable, is it good? Are you learning and growing through that? Is it training your brain to think more positive thoughts? And is it educating you? *Or, is it polluting you?*

Your brain stores data on a conscious level and on a subconscious level.
It's our forever computer. And we can't just get a new one, or totally wipe the hard drive.

Physical. What are you doing physically? We sit at computers a lot today, which is not the way our body was designed. We were designed to move about and be out in nature and be physical. It helps to get exercise, and get into nature. It depends on you, your schedule, your discipline level; whether you need a personal trainer, a workout buddy for accountability, or whether you are prepared to do that on your own.

We are all entitled to the pursuit of happiness, but the level of happiness really depends on us.
How sacred we are treating the space (our body) in which we live?

Nothing amazable comes without risk.
I grew up in a loving, safe home. My parents and teachers encouraged us to go for our dreams and our ambitions, so I was very blessed.

When I got into the workplace it was more challenging. Risky. There were men and women who may have been jealous, intimidated or who just misunderstood me. Some seemed to want to keep me under their control. That environment didn't feel very *safe*.

I had to continue to work on my leadership skills, too; on the things I greatly needed to improve. But, I also learned to ignore the people that wanted to be critical and the ones that didn't understand themselves – those who wanted to project their frustration and fear onto me.

I've stepped into yet another arena where some people are brilliant and empowering, and some are again coming from fear and insecurity. A friend of mine was running a Women's conference in Idaho, and when she retired her mission, she asked me if I was interested in creating Women's Conferences in Idaho. *Inside I thought, no flipping way!*

Never say never.
In my mind I was thinking I would not want to take on a massive project like that. In the American culture we're all so busy. Even unemployed and retired people are *busy*. #Interesting

Everybody's too busy.
We used to be double-booked in this culture ten years ago, and now we're quadruple-booked. We never seem to have enough time to get it all done.

I was busy, too, but one thing I have learned is: don't just shut down. Don't say *no* before you think and pray about it. It's easy to make mistakes by not even considering something simply because it hasn't been on our radar. *Oftentimes we don't allow even the possibility to come in.*

The first step of taking a risk is being open to the possibility of possibilities.
It doesn't cost you a dime to consider it. If it's your idea, or someone else's. Whether you had this concept, an idea as a kid, if it was a vision you had in a dream, a friend suggested it, or you read it in a book or in a blog,

If it's something positive, if it's something good; be open the possibility of possibilities. Be open to the thought that your dream is not just a dream, that it wasn't just a silly thought. We all have millions of ideas and thoughts, and certainly we can't do them all. But, sometimes there's that one that just keeps coming back. Sometimes we have an epiphany, a vision that really touches us on a visceral, deep level. If we go into that deeper self, we get an intuitive hit. We realize that *something is really speaking to me, I just keep thinking about this idea...*

Millions of inventions and ideas have come to people over time. Why not you?
Why can't *you* have the next best idea ever? Why can't you write the script that becomes the next blockbuster movie? Why can't you compose the symphony that goes down in time as a classic? Why can't you design the next dress that all the actresses want to wear? Why can't you run a faster mile than the guy with the record?

Everything starts with a thought.
Everything around us started with one person opening up their mind and their heart to the possibility that it could be. They realize they got a download, however it came, and it was meant to be. You don't have to know how it will all work out. Ideas don't initially come with road maps. *It's not that easy.*

The idea just comes as a thought. It knocks on your door and says, "Hey, are you open to the possibility of letting me live, letting me exist, and breathing life into me?" An idea doesn't have life without you. It cannot go anywhere without your legs, your mind, and your voice. *That idea needs you.*

Sometimes we think, "Well if I don't do it somebody else will; I don't need to create, I don't need to speak, or invent because somebody else will do what needs to be done on the planet, it's not me."

That's bogus.
There's even people that say, "God doesn't need us, He's got other people." I say that's a cop-out. He wouldn't have created me if He didn't need me. And, He wouldn't download in me the visions and thoughts He CHOSE to give me unless He entrusted them to me.

After you are open to the possibility, then let the seed germinate, let it be cultivated, and let it start to grow some sprouts. Then, start to dialogue with a friend about it; a safe, confidential friend that you respect. Go to a safe person, someone you trust and respect, and say, "I have an idea I want to run past you and I want to dialogue about it, and I just want to sit in the possibility of it."

Write about the possibilities.
Write in a secret, safe journal for your eyes only. You can tell your best friend where it is in case something happens to you. Journals are an amazing thing because they not only help unlock what's in our conscious mind, which is what we speak about, but what's underneath, in our subconscious as well.

When we write, we can take the filter off, turn the editor off, take expectations and judgements off; and just write, and write, and write. Write whatever you want. You don't even have to spell it right; *because it's just for you.*

As you write your ideas, you can begin to mind-map them. A mind map is a **diagram** used to visually organize information. Mind maps are often created around a central or main idea or concept, drawn as an image or word in the center of a page. Other ideas or categories branch out from the central concept.

Start with a circle in the middle of your page with your idea. Let's say it's an event. Put the word "EVENT" in the middle (it can be that generic to start with). Then, draw a circle around the word in the middle and draw a line coming from that circle. In another circle (attached to the new line) you can ideate...what kind of event do I want? Co-Ed? Community? Inspirational? Educational? And so, you start mind-mapping this thing out, writing down the words and thoughts that come to your mind without any editing and without any self-judging. You begin to build it. (See the mind map drawing in the back of the book for a visual)

As you journal, mind map, make lists, or as you're verbally processing ideas with your friend, do you notice things become just a little bit clearer and more in alignment? Do you notice your energy level going up? You still don't know all the *how*, but this idea's growing somehow. It's expanding, even just a little bit, with each baby step forward. It's growing, *it's becoming.*

Next you can sit down and start to write up a rough business plan, as a possibility.
Time to start a business plan. There are a ton of books, articles, videos, and classes on this. It's a great part of the building process, and it can lead you to next steps or to a mentor.

Don't be afraid to be afraid.
If you're afraid, that is good news. That means you're moving, trying, and growing. Excitement goes right along with it (adrenaline kicks in). And, you know what? It could be bigger than you even know. It could be so huge and ginormous. It could be the next Disneyland, the next Jolly Rancher candy, or it could

be a world-changing cure or cause. *It could be the next best-selling book.* Whatever it is, why not?

I'm crazy and courageous, and have enough faith to know that amazing, miraculous things happen when human beings get out of their own way.

Miracles happen in a moment, where our life is changed forever by one word, one event, or one person that comes into our life. In a moment the trajectory of our life is changed for eternity. You're on the front row to helping other people create miracles in their life. And, you're on the front row to your own miracles...*if you get out of the way.*

I was excited, and scared at times, and the Women Ignite Idaho conference started to pick up interest and traction. There were naysayers. No matter what you do, there's going to be loud and covert critics. People said things like, "You're just doing another women's event...we don't need another one of those." And, I would reply, "I'm not doing *another* event. I'm doing *this* women's event, and it's not like anything you've ever experienced."

This isn't just a business conference, this is the *what's next* of business conferences combined with dynamic Personal Transformation. *We bring in amazing entrepreneurs, thought leaders, and humanitarians and lives are literally changed- forever.*

Terilee and I brought a mini Ignite Conference to Ecuador as a *pay it forward* event. It was life changing. We shared real stories of courage and overcoming that touched many hearts.

Women Ignite (WI) International was born. All of the sudden, it went from being this one Idaho conference, to people wanting it across the country, and people are asking for us to bring WI to other cultures, too. Something is resonating.

Risk and the fear that comes with Risk can be almost debilitating.
Some days we're in our zone. But, other days, we get to learn how to move in spite of the fear and keep going, no matter what. Then, you can help your team overcome their own fears and insecurities, because they have them, too. Risk gets to happen. Start with the possibility. Let it grow and expand in you, if it continues to be something that resonates with you. And that's where *The Ignited Entrepreneur*, the ignited leader, the ignited humanitarian begins.

Might I suggest that we all risk at a level that God could then say; "Good work! I won't do for you what I have empowered you to do. You went. You trusted. You're giving it your all. Well done! *Now, I can bless you. I've been waiting for this moment…*"

Fuel for your flame:
What is your fear of risk, if any?
What area, idea or collaboration do you know that you need to take a bold step forward in?

Chapter 21: Vision
by Terilee

*Create the highest, grandest vision
for your life, because you become
what you believe. ~ Oprah Winfrey*

*Vision is oftentimes a hard thing for the brain to wrap around, but the
spirit understands very well. ~ Sheli G*

If your soul had an "Elevator Pitch" what would it say? ~ Sheli G

Hold the vision, trust the process.

I have worked with thousands of entrepreneurs over the years. When I think of an *Ignited Entrepreneur*, I can't help but think of one who stands out for *never* wavering in her vision for her business. Although she has been my boss for the last eight years (and one of my best friends), I'm not telling you about her to gain brownie points! Truly, this book would not be complete without telling you about Kelli Holmes, the Founder of TEAM Referral Network.

TEAM was first started in Southern California 13 years ago. From the beginning, Kelli had a vision of what she wanted her company to become. Through good times and bad, she has hung in there. I remember several years ago during tough economic times we watched so many of our business-owner friends give up and shut down their business to take a J-O-B or to try another business to see if that would work for them. Those times were not easy for us either, but giving up was absolutely *not* an option.

Kelli said, "From day one of starting TEAM Referral Network, I knew what I wanted it to be. I have certainly had ups and downs over the years in getting to this point, but today we stand close to my original vision, growing TEAM in ways that I only had in my imagination, but are now a reality. It has only been through faith (in God and myself), thinking big, sticking to it; surrounding myself with a good team, and always making *giving back* a priority that has allowed me to enjoy success. It's not easy being the one out at the end of a jetty, perched on the rocks, sometimes totally alone in the vision, knowing you're willing to risk just about anything to do what you are meant to do. Entrepreneurialism is certainly not for everybody, but it most definitely is for me."

We all need to know our vision, and to hold so tightly to it (myself included).

When you figure out your vision, let me know.
I'll never forget. I was at dinner with my friends, Nancy Burroughs and sales trainer, Eric Lofholm. Eric has been a mentor to Nancy and me for several years. I shared with Eric a bit about my story and my work helping people overcome shame. Eric asked me, "What is your vision?" I replied, "My vision? I'm not sure." He said, "When you figure it out, let me know."

I had always thought I was willing to follow God, and if I helped one person a day I was moving forward in my calling and doing a good thing. In searching my heart, I determined what I wanted my personal vision to be: *I want to help over one million people overcome shame in the next 25 years.*

The Message
What is your personal vision?

Establishing my vision has helped me to be more on point with my goals and the action I take each day.
I need to be "on it." I need to be developing programs to help an average of over 110 people each day. I still want to follow God's plan for me, but I am more determined now to think big, play big, *and help more people find freedom to love themselves and others.*

Why you need a personal vision.
When you have a personal vision in mind, you are more likely to accomplish much more than what you would otherwise. If you don't develop your own vision, you may find other people and circumstances tend to direct the course of your life.

Eric Lofholm recommends you create a personal vision so big you help others reach their vision inside of yours. If you help enough people get what they want, you will have everything you want. How can you include others inside your vision?

Here are some ideas:
Create a certification program.
Create an affiliate program.
Develop a way so others can train using your materials.

What would work for you? *Hint – plan backwards:*
What's the last thing that would've had to happen to achieve your best life?
What would you have learned?
What important actions would you have taken?
What beliefs would you have needed to change?
What habits or behaviors would you have had to cultivate?
What type of support would you have had to enlist?
How long will it have taken you to realize your best life?
What steps or milestones would you have needed to reach along the way?

Fuel for your flame:
What is your personal vision?
What can you develop inside your personal vision to help others reach their visions?

Chapter 22: Fear
by Sheli G

Fears can help you decide if something is worth doing. Befriend your fear. Feel it. Ask smart questions. Get objective feedback. And, if it's truly the right thing to do, then feel the fear and go anyway. ~ Sheli G

If fear shows up, pay attention. Fear often precedes real danger. Check it out, and trust your deepest intuition. ~ Sheli G

Here is the definition of fear according to Oxford Dictionaries Online Dictionary:

(Noun) an unpleasant emotion caused by the belief that someone or something is dangerous, likely to cause pain, or a threat: "drivers are threatening to quit their jobs in fear after a cabby's murder."
Synonyms: phobia · aversion · antipathy · dread · bugbear · nightmare

(Verb) third person present: fears · past tense: feared · past participle: feared · to be afraid of (someone or something) as likely to be dangerous, painful, or threatening: "he said he didn't care about life so why should he fear death?"
Synonyms: have a phobia about · have a horror of · take fright at

The Message
I hate the acronym that many still use for fear. I apologize in advance if it's your fave. But, I am speaking my truth.

F - False E - Evidence A - Appearing R - Real.

For one, it's been used a gabillion-trillion times, causing it to lose its impact and value. More importantly, I don't agree with this message, at all. #UnTruth

I have fear when my seven year old, incredibly impulsive son rushes out into a street (daily) before looking. Is that rational? YES! It's my job! My brain and body work together to allow me to respond to that fear, and attempt to keep him safe, as well as remind me how big my job is to teach him how to do that for himself. Having no fear for him in moments like that could be a deadly mistake.

I do agree that many people have fears about things, and they make the mistake of *marinating in their fears*. This doesn't help, solve, or soothe anything. It can, however, cement you in that fearful spot. If there's no value to what you're doing, I suggest a new approach. Now, *that* is a very logical, common-sense conversation.

If someone has fears that come from an irrational fear, like a phobia, anxiety, or mental illness, then logical conversations won't help. Don't waste your words of logic on someone trying to be their "breakthrough buddy" if they are coming from a strictly emotional or unstable space. It's not helpful, and it may even be hurtful to them, even if your intentions are good. If you, a loved one or a client is overcome by fears and cannot move past them, counseling is a great step. If someone has mental illness, depression or anxiety disorders, or possibly PTSD, (Post Traumatic Stress Disorder) I suggest getting at least a consultation. Choose a licensed counselor, who specializes in these areas and comes by way of a trustworthy referral.

Great questions to ask myself when I notice fear are, what does that mean? Do I need to be cautious? Do I need to investigate the credibility of someone or something in business or life? Am I or is someone or something in danger – physically, emotionally, financially, spiritually, relationally, psychologically, or other-wise? Am I being irrational, overly emotional or immature? Am I being judgmental? Am I being triggered because this reminds me if someone or something from my past? Is a control issue showing up? Is the risk too great? Am I just outside of what I know and am comfortable with? Have I had too much coffee? (Yes!)

Before I speak or sing, I always have fear. That little voice in my head that implies what if? Sheli, what if you "swan dive" on your face in front of all of these people who are expecting great things from you? This real emotion occurs at almost every event where I am featured.

I used to get extremely sick to my stomach as a child before I sang a solo. No one ever knew, except my mother.

In college, I was sitting in the front row of a chapel service getting ready to sing. I was very nervous. It was fear, and it was real. The older Alumnus sitting next to me could tell I had some anxiety. She leaned over and said "Honey, are you afraid?" I looked at her and said, "Absolutely!" She smiled through her adorable wrinkles and said with that sage kind of wisdom tone, "Well good. You should be. This is the highest honor, to sing for God! Don't ever take it for granted."

That really hit home, and made a long-term, significant impact on me. I noticed that I still felt the fear, but I had a deeper knowing of the why beneath my fear, and it was okay. I *should* feel nervous! I *should* double-check my authenticity meter, my humility factor, and not take this moment for granted. Feel the fear, and go anyway. *It turned into adrenaline for me, excitement, and joy simultaneously as I sang.*

If we allow those emotions to dance together, we don't have to stay locked down in fear. Fear can be friended. If you're starting a new business, I suggest you allow some fear. Too many people jump in without a plan. They jump in without what they need. They jump in because someone told them they should. They misunderstand the financial, time, and emotional investments a business needs. They don't calculate the risks. They don't do enough market research. They feel invincible.

Don't run into the busy street called Entrepreneurial Avenue without looking both ways first. Feel the real fear factor, or you may get smooshed by the ignited train barreling down the avenue towards you instead of with you. The only good news in that case is that you will learn.

If you do your due diligence, and yet you feel a calling anyway... if you know the risks and you feel the fear yet you know this has to be...if you have mentors or coaches in your life to objectively help you navigate this process...then feel the fear and go anyway.

Fuel for your flame:
Have you taken bold risks in your life?
What is the payoff to taking a risk you know you were meant to take?
What is the risk if you fail to take it, when you know you are meant to?

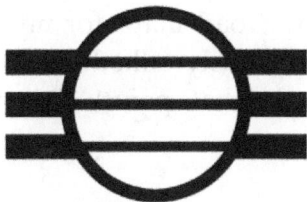

Chapter 23: Focus
by Sheli G

The best leaders not only focus on an objective, they hyper-focus. They are unflinchingly sold out to attaining the result they are targeting, and will do everything healthy that is called forth to achieve their end goal.
~ Sheli G

Focus means to set attention on or to bring sharply into view. In the Gallup Strengthsfinder's© books, Gallup defines the strength of Focus as: "Focused people who are strong in the Focus theme can take a direction, follow through, and make the corrections necessary to stay on track. They prioritize, then act."

The Message

Think of your finest hour, your best project or task where you really shined. Usually, it takes hard work, strategic planning, and some consistent, clear *focus* on what you are working on to achieve the objective.

I can think of a time when my focus was not very clear, and the results at least in my mind, were less than phenomenal. I was asked to speak to a women's group on social media. My talk was entitled "Rising Above the Noise."

I was originally given 40 minutes to share, but several circumstances intervened, and at the last moment I found out I only had about 15 minutes to share. It's really not long enough to tackle that massive topic. Not even close! And, I had a PowerPoint with a lot of dynamic content, and a focused flow, which only confused the matter.

What do I cut? Do I start the PowerPoint and skip a bunch in the middle? What's the most important, valuable information to laser focus in on and share? Well, it all happened so fast that I did not have time to establish a new "road map" for my talk. I should have just gone in and spontaneously talked about a few keys that are the most important at that point! This is my specialty.

I did my best at that time with what I had. I used part of my PowerPoint. For me, my lack of focus as I winged it showed up. I did not feel I led them to a clear destination point. I gave some good points and left them with a great quote. I did not do my personal goal, which at every gig, I knock out of the park! Sigh...

Now compare that to talks I have done where I know all the criteria, logistics and times, I'm really prepared, and everything goes off seamlessly...WOW! My intention can really focus in. I can open well, do a crowd warm up, take them into my material, leave them with a more complete package, and give them a call to action to implement positive change in their businesses, their relationships, or their lives. Now that feels good, and I can tell a huge difference in where they "land" at the end of the session. My clarity produces clarity for everyone else! Bam!

This happened at our Women Ignite Idaho Conference the first year we held it. Everyone said I was crazy, that we didn't need *another women's conference*, and that I would lose big money. Well, I made money. We accomplished everything we set out to do and more. When the participants left, their feedback said it was the most life-changing experience ever. They said the speakers were beyond inspirational. The results met and exceeded our expectations. *But, that was my goal.*

If the leader or leadership isn't clear and focused in where they want to go with a team or project, why they want to go there, and how to make that happen, the team will certainly feel, see, and experience that on some level.

It takes a passionate, focused vision.
It takes intense strategic planning, before, during and ongoing in

your venture. It takes consistency and fierce discipline, that no matter what, you get up, show up, and do whatever needs to be done to further your business or cause. You have to know or learn how to just "plug your nose and go" no matter what the weather, the economy, your emotions, your bank account, your associates and employees are saying. You get to be willing to ride out the lows as well as enjoy the highs. Focus. Entrepreneurship isn't easy. It's a calling. It's a lifestyle. It's the hardest and best job on earth for the committed.

Fuel for your flame:
What are the top three things right now that I need to focus on? Are there any distractions that I can cut out right now, (people, places or things) so that my focus on what is important becomes easier to maintain?

Chapter 24: Anxiety
by Sheli G

Worry and fear serve as warning signs: either you shouldn't do something (if fear is helping you make sound choices), OR it's a sign that you worry often, about even common things, and it may be time to reach out for healthy ways to get your fears under control. ~ Sheli G

If you use up all your best energy in worry or fear, are you in alignment with your purpose? Getting worry in check not only leaves you with more joy and peace, it frees up the World Changer in you to fulfill what you came to this planet to do. We cannot truly serve others, unhinged and full throttle, when we're stuck in fear. ~ Sheli G

Anxiousness. Worry. Fear.
My friend, Bradley, tells the story of the day he learned about anxiety. He was ten years old and his stepfather was the principal at the grade school he attended. Being a ten year old boy, Bradley made a mistake and had to go to the principal's office to receive his reprimand. He was anxious about going because he knew his stepfather would be doubly disappointed in him. He dreaded walking down the big, echoing hall to the main office. He tells the story that he took his reprimand and learned his lesson about being disruptive in class. He also learned about being anxious. That wrenching fear of the unknown...the anticipation of reprimand.

Another story about anxiety comes from my friend, Dave, who became so anxious about speaking in front a crowd of his peers, that he became sick and ended up losing his lunch, so to speak, before he walked up to speak. He made it through, but it was a horrifying few days before the actual event happened, fraught with fear and anxiety.

We've all been there on varying levels. Anxiety comes when it pleases, in small or massive ways. It can have a "Take No Prisoners" flavor to the emotion.

The Message

I think it's healthy for leaders to understand that concept of "To whom much is given, much is expected." This is a philosophy most people believe worldwide. As leaders, we are steering people towards something, and with most leaders it's usually the light or the dark.

So, a certain amount of responsibility and pressure that innately comes with this leadership is to be expected. *But, when anxiety tips your scale, you can see the challenging results.*

I remember a day in one of my earlier entrepreneurial pursuits, when as an owner of a Mortgage Brokerage company, I had to fire a guy. He had no production, he committed fraud (to mention only a couple of the issues) and he had filed suit against us. Not only did he sue my company, he hit me with a personal lawsuit as well, attempting to *pierce the corporate veil.*

Seeing my own birth name on that ugly, legal document full of huge lies, and realizing our laws let crazy people like him do this without proof or cause at-will, *that* gave me some true anxiety.

Some things are completely out of our control, and shake us to our core.
Some things are a direct or indirect result or consequence of a choice we have made. Perhaps these are the worst instances of anxiety, when we know it's in some way our fault. We wonder, could it have been avoided? Relationship challenges. Financial hardship. Health issues. *There is no shortage of challenges and the emotions that accompany them, for all of us to learn how to navigate.*

I work with an alarming amount of people who deal with some moderate to extreme versions of anxiety. Again, this usually stems from people having bad things happen to them, or poor choices made, or both, and a lack of training and permission to navigate these issues, so that they can "un-hook" from the chains that bind them. Also stress, lack of sleep, poor diet, poor company and addictions can add to the challenge of anxiety. If you are struggling with anxiety, I believe counseling can be very beneficial. Find a therapist you really connect with and let it all out. *Get a referral from someone you trust.*

Also, I have found in some of the personal and business development workshops I facilitate, that with proven processes, gifted facilitators, and authentic willingness from the participants, you can achieve full-blown miracles! I have watched thousands of men and women get honest about these blocks or "dragons" in their lives. I have seen them pro-actively tackle these issues, and come out the other side conquerors over their fears, anxieties, and their past. This not only allows you to find freedom, it educates you on how to support your family, friends and your team better as you learn to navigate these difficulties with confidence.

Anxiety can often come with a partner called Depression. There are self-assessments you can use to determine if you may be dealing with either Anxiety issues and/or Depression, in minor, moderate or major levels.

Go to this link to do a basic Depression self-assessment: webmd.com/depression/depression-assessment

Use this link to do a basic Anxiety level self-assessment: psychcentral.com/quizzes/anxiety.htm

There are other online self-assessments and tools, so Google and check the source. This does not formally diagnose you in any way, but may just let you know if you or someone you love needs to seek professional help. *When in question, it's best to seek a professional consultation, always.*

If you find you are dealing with any level of anxiety and/ or Depression, it's really a great idea to get a referral to an awesome counselor or therapist in your area and go deeper.

If you or someone you know is beyond your ability or helping skill level with anxiety and/or Depressive symptoms, either call 911 or take them to the ER. You can get stabilized, and then begin to get to the core reasons that you are feeling this way. *There is always help and hope, it's just about reaching out. There are answers. You're not alone.*

Fuel for your flame:
What makes you the most anxious?
Does worry or anxiety ever get in the way of your work or relationships?

Chapter 25: Excitement
by Terilee

Excitement is the fuel for your flame of calling or purpose for your life.
~ Terilee Harrison

What positive thing, action or goal really excites you? Is it valuable not only to you, but to others? Then do that, often! ~ Sheli G

Living the life of an entrepreneur excites me! Does it excite you?

Excitement is defined as:
to arouse or stir up (emotions or feelings): to excite purpose.
to cause; awaken: to excite interest or curiosity.
to stir to action; provoke or stir up: to excite an entrepreneur into action.

The Message
You've been there...You pitch your business and the prospective client "likes you" and "gets it" and they "want it" and they enroll in your program or hire you. Let's face it, success is exciting!

Excitement IS the fuel for your flame of calling and purpose for your life. It will get you up in the morning, help you take brave actions to move yourself forward each day, and keep your dream alive!

Here are some of the many things you may find exciting about your entrepreneurial life:

Being true to yourself, and living out your purpose or calling is exciting.
In the moments when you live out your calling and you know in your soul you are doing the right thing and are in your sweet spot, now that is exciting. Our callings are different and so are

our stories about what *being true to yourself* looks like, but when it happens, you KNOW it. There is nothing better than that.

Freedom.
Being free to create your own schedule is exciting.
I have worked a corporate job with Monday-Friday, 8 to 5 hours. I did this for years. I adore being in charge of creating my own life and schedule. Sure, there might be times when I work more than 40 hours a week, but there are times when I don't. I get to homeschool my son and that time is priceless to me. What is priceless to you in your schedule?

Working toward financial freedom is exciting.
As an entrepreneur, you have the ability to grow your business toward unlimited levels of income. In the beginning, there is the working hard and dreaming big that has to happen. The journey is exciting and worth it.

Connecting with others.
Helping others is exciting.
Whether you are a plumber and you help people unclog their drains, a life coach who helps people to transform their lives, or a realtor who helps people get into their first home, it is exciting to help people get what they need in life. Exciting. Rewarding. Fulfilling. Satisfying.

Meeting new people is exciting.
Extroverts might find meeting new people more exciting than introverts do, but ask yourself as you meet someone new: How can I help this person? Could I introduce them to someone I know that could help them in some way? Might I be able to do business with them? Perhaps they might do business with me? Could we become friends? You never know what can happen when you meet someone new!

Collaboration is exciting.
Collaboration is taking the excitement of meeting someone new to an entirely new level! Collaboration with another professional

is amazing because there is twice the brainpower, twice the heart, twice the soul, twice the sizzle, and possibly twice the audience that can come from your project. Who can you collaborate with on your next project?

Enrolling others in your vision is exciting.
I love supporting other business owners in their vision. Our dreams are all so important. This journey of entrepreneurship is a serious matter. There is nothing like the moment when someone says, "Meeting you changed my life," or "Being involved in your organization is what saved my business" to excite your entrepreneurial soul.

New things.
Ideas are new and exciting. There is nothing like a new idea to get an entrepreneur excited. It could be a new logo. Maybe it's a new website. A new program. *Maybe it's an industry game changer.* #Woohoo

Possibilities are exciting.
What *if* your new program *is* an industry game changer? How many people could you help? How would it feel to be financially free?

Growing and expanding both as an individual and professional is exciting.
There is nothing like knowing where you have come from and being able to celebrate how far you have come. Sometimes you take little steps and sometimes you take giant leaps, but each step is a miracle toward becoming the person you were meant to be.

Achieving goals is exciting.
Have you ever set a goal and blown it? (That has never happened to me! LOL) All the more reason for being excited when you do achieve a goal that you set! You are doing big things. It's cause to celebrate each and every time.

Long-term thinking.
Leaving a legacy for your family is exciting. Why do you do what you do? Do you want to do more for your family now? Do you want to leave behind a business you can pass onto your family?

The entrepreneurial life certainly has ups and downs. Your excitement can help to carry you through during challenging times.

Handling challenges with grace and ease is exciting.
The life of a business owner is full of ups and downs. There are times when you will be hurt, burnt, or just plain tired out. When this happens, ask yourself:
What lesson can be learned from this circumstance?
How can I keep this from happening again?
How can I handle this with grace? Sometimes getting mad and over-reacting is not the answer.

Risk is exciting.
There is certainly a downside to risk, and sometimes it does not pay off. The upside of risk as an entrepreneur and the potential payoff of it is totally exciting. What if you've lost your excitement for your business? Can you get it back? Sometimes life happens. It can drain you. Or new interests can pull you from the spark you had for your business. I am here to tell you that you can get your excitement for your business back! You can choose back in. Recommit to your business, your dream, your goals, and serving your clients. *You may be surprised how your results and outcomes will change.*

Fuel for your flame:
What are the top three things that excite you as an entrepreneur? How can I raise my excitement level to keep my flame continually fueled?

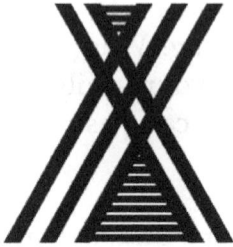

Chapter 26: Liability
by Sheli G

The biggest risk is not taking any risk. In a world that changes so quickly, the only strategy guaranteed to fail is not taking risks. ~ Mark Zuckerberg

Don't worry about liability or risk. Instead, take proactive actions to protect yourself. Get professionals who are trusted masters of what they do to have your back and your business' well-being. In other words, don't jump out of the plane without a great parachute. It's worth it.
~ Sheli G

Liability – eewww. The very word itself is what I refer to as a *restrictive* word (versus an expansive one). It conjures up all kinds of fear, worry, and thoughts of dollar amounts lost in the mere mention.

The Message
It's true...an entrepreneur has liability. It's your name on the paperwork, the listing, the sign, and the website. You have the responsibility, even if it's just what someone under you does or says. Once you own it, you own it: profit and loss, reputation and otherwise. There's the hard ownership – the assets, products and patented services, and the soft ownership – everything else that happens that can somehow affect you.

One can never understand that feeling; the ultimate "buck stopping with me" that comes with ownership, and all the highs and lows that accompany the ride, *until you've experienced it personally.*

I remember one night when I owned the mortgage business, some of our employees were going to have a drink after work. Harmless enough, one might think. But, they left with our work logo shirts on. I was nervous. What if? What if they drove after drinking? What if they were in an accident and there they were, on the late night news, in *our* shirts. What if they were in a bar fight, forgot to pay their tab, went home with a stranger...? What or how does that reflect on us?

Social media really changes the way employers and organizations look at employees and volunteers. What are they posting about the company, or the clients, or personally? Rumors, scandals and slanderous words, videos and pictures abound. This adds up to a company or public figure's worst nightmare, potentially.

This is why employers more and more look you up online before (or during) your employment or volunteering to see what you represent and communicate. I have helped various companies over the years with interviewing, hiring and firing, and it's happening more frequently now. People are not getting the job or they are getting reprimands, or losing their jobs over their personal messaging.

For better or worse, depending on your product or service, employees or volunteers' social pages may become an extension of your company's messaging. It's important to address this upfront in interviews, job contracts, offers and reviews, setting crystal clear policies, procedures and expectations, both hard and soft.

If you have an HR manager and or department, they must be really up on internet liability to truly support you and your team members.

There are other risks, too.

When I first opened my mortgage brokerage business, I received some sound and timely advice from my financial planner. He was reviewing my auto insurance, because I heard that you need that reviewed by an expert when you own a business, as your risks and liabilities change dramatically.

The day of our meeting, I increased my coverage. I also listened as he told me to be careful in regards to accidents now that I was a business owner. Within a week of that visit, I was on a dark road, which was covered in black ice. One car was in front of me. We were the only two cars in sight, as far as I could see. The road went on for miles.

Suddenly, and without any cause that I could see, the driver in front of me slammed on his brakes. His red brake lights beamed through the otherwise dark road, and didn't let up. No stoplight, stop sign or other cars were the catalyst for this. I reacted the same way, slamming on my brakes full force, and praying. But, with the black ice acting as a thin film turning the road into an ice rink, I could see I wasn't going to be able to fully stop in the middle of this road in time. Without the ice it would have been no problem.

Then, I noticed a dog run to the other side of the road. *Oh, that's why he was stopping – a dog.* He clearly wasn't aware that my car slamming into the back of his car could have hurt us both much more! All of this happened in seconds.

Since that meeting with my auto insurance agent, his advice flashed through my entrepreneurial brain... "Sheli, avoid hitting other cars if you safely can! If they find out you're a business owner, some people will take advantage of that, acting like they have more injuries, even suing you AND your company, too." Yikes!

I acted quickly, noticing a field to my right, and no fence, cars or people...just a field and a way to avoid crashing into this car in front of me. I could avoid hurting him and myself. I could probably minimize damage to my car and avoid damaging his. Perfect.

My pretty, limited edition Camry had some damage, but I was very happy with my decision. It was better and safer for all involved, and I was happy for two reasons: that I had set a meeting with my insurance agent that empowered me to understand my risks, and thrilled that the meeting led to an awareness that helped me make a split second, potentially life and business-saving action.

In my mortgage business I had a partner. We were well matched in many ways, as we had different strengths. Good partnerships are built on this foundation. You deserve to have a common-goals philosophy and integrity – those are your partnership glue. And, when partners bring different strengths, experiences, education, and abilities to the table, you will have a much better shot at success.

That said, those different gifts we all bring to the table mean you risk having to replace their strengths if your partner(s) becomes ill, injured, disabled or dies. Thankfully, there is insurance to cover such events. It takes proactive research of the company and policies available, but it may save your business.

For example, I had "Key Man Life Insurance" on my partner, who happened to be my dad! So imagine, tragedy strikes and my father dies...not only would our business have suffered a huge loss in both production and administrative tasks that he facilitated, but I would have clearly needed time off, and who knows how much, to grieve, have services, get some personal support and finally get back to work.

Who could take our place? A nice-sized policy helps you cover the losses incurred financially, and possibly could help you make a nice offer to a new partner to come aboard your company (either temporarily or full time) that otherwise you may not be able to afford. *Don't leave yourself vulnerable when emotional loss strikes. The financial stress takes you out of the game.*

My CPA makes all the difference in our taxes. He knows every in and out, what to do and what *not* to do. My liability of getting audited goes down, and I have an advocate to stand with me and coach me through it if I do. Don't try to do this alone unless you are a master of it. That's my best tax advice. *They will usually save you more money, time and headaches than you spend hiring a great CPA.*

Getting the right attorney is also paramount.

I learned this the hard way. We had an attorney who was okay at some paperwork (like employee contracts), but when we got sued by a crazy former employee, our attorney really dropped the ball. I found out only after her huge error, that she was more skilled (supposedly) in real estate law versus employee/employer matters.

She received a faxed letter saying if we didn't respond by X date, we would be sued, but she failed to notify *us*. So, we were in the middle of a bogus suit that we still paid tens of thousands of dollars to fight and defend before we had a chance to contemplate more proactive options. I fired her and hired an expert for this type of case. He was great. I only wish I would have known sooner that we had the wrong representation to start with. A costly lesson not only financially, but even more so emotionally. *Don't make our mistake your learning curve. Have a plan, including an expert in place beforehand.*

I am not an insurance agent, a CPA, or an attorney, *but I know the right masters in these fields are worth gold to you and your business.*

Fuel for your flame:

What kind of risk do you have or do you imagine you will have in your business or industry?
What experts, in order of priority, should you interview to assist you?

Chapter 27: Responsibility by Terilee

When you take responsibility and own up to what you have done, it can bring healing to you and to others. ~Terilee Harrison

More people would learn from their mistakes if they weren't so busy denying them. ~ Harold J. Smith

Responsibility and the Christmas Nails

This is a text conversation between Sheli G and Terilee: (Terilee sends a pic of her new red Christmas nails with Santa hand-painted on them)

T: My nail guy begged me to let him do a design today. Show Teisha (Sheli's daughter).

S: I know what you mean. My nail guy has to beg me to do designs, too. lol

T: I wasn't expecting Santa, but now I've got to be festive.

S: Lol

The next day: (Sheli sends picture of her new, deep burgundy nails with a rhinestone cross on them)

T: Okay now. I was thinking I needed a cross. That looks a bit dark for you, yes?

S: But you chose Satan, er I mean Santa, instead. Yes it's dark. Like Jesus' blood. I'm very spiritual today. :)

T: Hahaha. Nice. I didn't choose.

S: I know. He (the nail tech) held a gun to your head. Right?

T: Next time I will clarify what design he is excited to make. My Sunday school kids will be all over this. I can use this as a story for the responsibility chapter. (Pause.) Or not.

S: You be the whimsy of Christmas. I'll be the depth.

T: Okay

S: Yes. Take some responsibility.

The Message

You need to be responsible *all* the time, even if it's at your nail appointment. I don't mind Santa on my nails for a few weeks during December, but the next time my nail guy wants to do a design, I will either tell him what I want or ask him what he wants to do...*before* he starts.

Sometimes your issues with responsibility can be way more serious than ending up with Santa on your nails.

How can this keep happening to me?
There was a time in my life when I didn't claim responsibility for a lot of things. I operated in victim mode and created a big fat mess in my personal life that kept spilling over into my business.

How did I end up in a relationship with a man who was so mean and controlling?
How could he have lied to me about everything?
Why did I have to put up with his abuse?

Do you see the difference?

Responsibility is the state of being accountable for something within one's power or control.

To take responsibility, you need to own what you've done. Here's the thing about owning your mistakes: Do you worry about what others will think of you? *What if they won't like me? They don't know what I've done.*

Truthfully, we all make mistakes. You may have made the same mistakes as me. You may have made different mistakes. No one is perfect. When you take responsibility and own up to what you have done, it is inspiring to others. It can bring healing to you and to others.

Taking responsibility for being exactly where you are gives you the power to be exactly where you want to be. How many business owners found themselves drowning in deep financial waters in 2009-2011? Were you one of them? How did you handle that challenge? How have you handled other challenges?

Fuel for your flame:

What actions do I need to accept responsibility for?
How can I take ownership of my mistakes?
How can I be accountable for results?

Chapter 28: Passion
by Sheli G

Passion is the genesis of genius.
~ Galileo Galilei

There is no passion to be found playing small – in settling for a life that is less than the one you are capable of living. ~ Nelson Mandela

If they don't really want to build a company, they won't luck into it. That's because it's so hard that if you don't have a passion, you'll give up. ~ Steve Jobs

"Everyone has passion. It's a matter of knowing what you're passionate about. Unlock, activate and move forward from that space. ~ Sheli G"

I think passion has to be one the best words in the English language. I just love it. I think the word embodies what I feel inside so often, *and what I didn't really recognize for so long. It was my passion.*

The Message
When I hear people say, "I'm such a passionate person," I think, *great. Wait, we are ALL passionate!* The way we express it might look different, or the way that we channel that into the directions and the trajectory of our lives can look and show up and sound very different. *But, after working with people in so many capacities, and so deeply for all these years, it's what I know.*

When passion is unlocked, activated, and fully mobilized, it's unstoppable.
It's just a matter of finding out what *you* are passionate about. What gets you fired up? What lights you up, making every cell in your body come alive and be inspired?

When I was younger, my passion often overwhelmed people. I'm sure that it was partly due to not understanding myself well yet, or how to articulate my passion, and not moving with it in a way that was fluid to enroll the people around me.

It's true...sometimes my passion can be perceived as over-whelming, especially due to some of my other strengths and gifts, like the achiever in me, the urgent go-do-be part of me. The way I naturally show up in the world, since I was tiny, can be pretty bold, non-PC, dramatic, bright, with the volume turned up. *And, at times, they say, my passion can be intimidating to some people.*

However it shows up, I believe that passion is really important for *The Ignited Entrepreneur.*
The Ignited Entrepreneur isn't usually the one who owns their business because they were just handed it. They're not one who seems apathetic, or one who owns a business but doesn't really care, isn't inspired by it, and aren't very inspiring to others. That's not who we are.

There are many things we can all do to simply make money, but we don't have to be passionate about those things. Do with your business whatever's important to you, whether that's making money, making a difference or a product that makes our life easier, or connecting people to other people. *There's so many ways that we can be of true value.*

But, if somebody's only doing something to make a buck, it's not usually inspiring. It's also difficult to do that year after year, decade after decade if you're not passionate about it, if you don't love it on some level, *if it doesn't light you up.*

At some point we say people have what we like to call a "midlife crisis," but I think it's more of a crossroads many of us reach in our time. We get older. We get wiser. Life experiences happen, and we start to think, *wow! I think there's more to my life than this,* or *I want there to be more to my life than this because,* as Jack Nicholson said in one of his movies…**"Is this as good as it gets?"**

It's a very good question to ask ourselves, and many of the clients I have life coached do. In your work, your humanitarian efforts, your philanthropic efforts, in the circles of friends you have, and the activities that you do, we may start to feel like, "Eh, this doesn't do it for me anymore! Maybe I've grown out of or past it. Maybe that was a chapter or a time in my life, but now I need the *what's next*. I need to evolve and adapt and come to this moment in time, and *what am I really passionate about, right now?"*

That's not a midlife crisis. That's a breakthrough.
Whenever this happens to you, it's growth and enlightenment. It's good news! Sometimes our passions *do* change, and that means our pursuits change. *Today looks completely different than what I was passionate about 5, 10, 15 years ago.*

There are so many dynamics that change throughout our lives, and we have the opportunity to change as well.
I think who we are is pretty innate. It's in there when we mine it and cultivate it. But, the *who we are* can become more clear, more developed, and more passionate over the years as we get better at finding out what our passion is. We gain more understanding and knowledge about how we deliver that passion, and enroll other people into it in a healthy, productive and valuable way that works, *not just for us, but for others.*

Hopefully my passion fires up my community, and has a reverberating ripple effect that can move into the world.
One way I've noticed the evolution of passion within myself is that I had the honor of growing up in a family that were speakers, teachers, singers, and preachers. What a wonderful opportunity for me. Most people have a fear of public speaking, but it was normal to me. Now, swimming in the same body of water as sharks on the other hand…no thanks! #NotThatCrazy

I'm sure that was no accident that God had me in this family, because it's the calling on my life to use those modalities to get my message to the world. The message on my heart, my purpose is to:

Inspire other people to unlock their greatest passion, their purpose, their cause, their calling and to help them move through the obstacles that might be in their way. To give people inspiration and hope, and to be a catalyst of encouragement, edification, affirmation, and bold truth to people.

The stage is a great platform for me to do that. It's just a vehicle. It's not about ego or trying to be famous. The only thing I think that's cool about being famous, is that you have a great ability (and responsibility) *to influence in a big way with your positive, healthy, holy message to the world if you choose.*

I think it's very important that to whom much is given, that they deliver with great integrity and great responsibility to the people who might be hearing their message.

Because of this, I'm very honored by the platform of a stage, whatever size it is and wherever it is. I want to go where I'm called to go. I want to speak to who I'm supposed to speak to. *I want to encourage and help them in whatever way that I can.*

I am lucky that growing up, it was not only normal to be stage speaking, but also singing, coming from your heart, coming from purpose, passion and above all, serving. Coming from a place of serving others and not making it about you, but *having your message be about the encouragement and the support of others, is powerful.*

Passion doesn't erase the need for us to work on our craft. You can still passionately suck.

Even with your innate talent, a calling (a divine purpose), and even with your passion unlocked, you still get to work, gain experience, get education, practice, be mentored, and receive constructive feedback. Skipping steps will only lead to more failures and bloody noses along the way. Those are good for learning, too, *but we all get to earn our stripes to master our giftings.* #Ouch

Constructive feedback is sometimes very difficult.
And even so, you deserve to hear it, to get better, and become more effective at delivering your message. It deserves to be the best that it can be, *so that distractions are moved out of the way.*

It's not about being perfect, but it is about being grounded, comfortable, graceful, and fluid about the *way* that you deliver your message to ensure *the message isn't inhibited.*

I got into drama classes, speech classes and debate classes during high school and college. Every single one of them presented profound opportunity, fear, experience, and excellent teachers who were placed in my path. *And still, every single time I speak, I learn something.*

As long as there's breath in my body, I want to learn, grow, and get better.
Even with all my passion, I have had a bunch of talks or speeches I wish I could hit a "re-do" button on. There were times I thought about it critically for days, even weeks after; times I wished I had prepared more or knew more, and that just comes with more time, praying and training. It took a long time to feel like I could say to myself, "That message was clear, bold and really delivered well." And, there are still always things I want to "dial up." There have been many times, as with any craft or skill that we're learning, that I have felt like, "Wow, I've got a long way to go." And, that was the truth. There were some gaping holes. There were things I missed. There were important things that I really did want to serve this particular audience with, but got left out. Again, welcome to your greatest teacher: experience. *Experience is one of passion's best teachers, and you can't skip it.*
#YouCan'tAvoidIt

Experience will teach and preach like no book or mentor will.
The books, training, mentors, school, teachers, and your abilities
are important. We learn in so many ways, but we're very
experiential learners. When we DO, when we put into action,
risk, and GO, the lessons go deep very quickly – what worked,
what didn't work, *and what we can do better next time.*

**All the ways we learn are paramount for the things we cannot
prepare for.** What happens if…
At one point I stood up to speak at a large gala event in
California, and there was no podium. There was no place to put
my notes. I'm not a tied-to-my-notes person, yet I had some that
day just to keep me on track. It was just fine though, because I
knew how to adapt at that point in my career. The preparation
was great, and what I was going to present was great, and my
confidence afforded me the ability to let go of that minor concern
and go up there ready to rock. *I've prepared, I feel grounded, and I
can speak from that space in the moment something valuable and true,
from my spirit, without the notes.*

**Being passionate isn't enough. You need to master your
giftings.**
When is it *too* much passion though? Have you ever wondered
that? Or, been accused of that? I reached a point when I had to
ask myself: How do I stay authentic and true to who I am and
not let other people diminish me by saying, "You're just too
much. You've got to dial it way back…" Where's the line when
everything inside my spirit wants to leap out and speak boldly;
to speak messages of truth that are difficult to deliver sometimes,
even messages people may not want to hear?

How do I be me and not be so worried that everybody's going to
be overwhelmed? As we continue to work with people and
understand people better, we learn how to do the dance of being
our authentic selves and also compassionately holding them in
the place that they are at, simultaneously: *finding that balance.*

Every group or situation can be energetically different, and I can adapt to a little bit of that environment, without changing who I am and feeling like I'm being inauthentic. There are certainly spaces and places where I feel I can spread my wings full on, and times I dial it back. *Mirroring the people around you can help with this.*

I believe that you have a passion inside of you. The only question is what are you passionate about? What are you really excited about?

Maybe it's a product that you really believe it makes a difference or makes life easier. Maybe it makes our health better, assists people in some way, or makes life more exciting and fun. Maybe you're passionate about finding a cure for something or helping to stop an injustice that's happening. Maybe that's what gets you really fired up, and you notice that you talk passionately when you discuss that certain topic. Or, if you're posting on a social media platform, you notice causes and conversations that rile you up, and you want to stand for it, and you want to be a voice that will help to propel something forward or educate people in some way.

Maybe you're passionate about teaching people something. You're passionate about showing other people how to do something, because you're just really good at teaching people a way where they are frustrated otherwise.

If you haven't found your passion or purpose yet, I just want to encourage you. You still can.
You didn't pick up *The Ignited Entrepreneur* by accident. Somebody gave this to you, or you saw it and it called out to you. There's something in you that either is ignited and is on the hunt for the support and the resources to take it to the highest levels that you deserve to go, *or you want something inside of you to be ignited.* Even if you just want something to be ignited and you're not sure what that is yet, be excited anyway. Today you

are on the path to finding it.

There's a light that's lit, and it just wants to be turned up and expanded into its fullness.
Sometimes that takes seeking and asking the right questions in the right places; safe places, healthy places, places and people where you go to for wisdom (like to mentors or wise, grounded people that have gone before you).

As we seek, sometimes we find our own answers. Sometimes when we verbally process things, journal things, watch documentaries, YouTube videos, read books, or go to online or in-person classes for development...epiphanies come.

Breakthroughs come when we least expect it.
Remember, one moment can change everything. One day, one meeting with someone new, one idea, one billboard that you drive past can give you that lightning rod moment where something shifts inside. In that instant you figure out what your passion is, or you figure out where to let your passion unlock into or what your passion is supposed to support, create or propel forward in the world. *So, I just want to encourage you.*

Stay on the journey. Stay in the question.
Questions are good, because at some point they get answered. If you keep asking the questions—again, ask them in a safe place with healthy, safe people, and find modalities that are great for teaching you—and you continue to risk and look like a fool for your passion, at some point we've got to move. Quit researching and waiting and go-do-try. Do, try and be some things that are out of your comfort zone; some things that we haven't tried before. Then we have a moment. We have *that* moment, *that* day, or a friendship or a business connection, and we get it.

We get ignited, the flame starts to grow, and the impurities burn off as that flame gets hotter.
As we get more clarity, more direction, education, and more practice, we fine tune – we hone in. *We find the direction in which*

our passion is supposed to go.

Don't ever let anybody tell you you're too passionate. Nobody's ever too passionate.
Don't ever let yourself think that passion isn't a good thing, because passion is critical, and it's so amazing. It can make you feel so alive, and it can be much of the fuel that propels us to do the things that we need to do, that we want to do, the things that matter, that make a difference.

Things that make a difference aren't easy. Most of our callings, our work, or our causes take work. It takes commitment and consistency, even when you don't feel like it, and even when it's tough. Even if the people around you become naysayers at some point and don't get it, *don't ever sell out on what you're passionate about.*

Don't ever sell out on trying to find and unlock your passion, because it's important.
It matters, and as long as you have breath in you, you can do it. As long as you're alive, you can do something with passion that you've been born with. It may be very unique what you do with it or how you do it, but just trust the process. Trust yourself, and when you know, that you know, that you know you've found a way to release your passion in a healthy, positive way, then you just go for it.

Fuel for Your Flame:
What are you the most passionate about in life?
Are you living in your passion with your business or cause?
Do you ever feel that you have to scale back your passion?

Chapter 29: Communication
by Terilee

Speak in such a way that others love to listen to you.
Listen in such a way others love to speak to you. ~ Unknown

We are always communicating; with our words, or lack of words. With our body language, our clothing, our voice intonation, and our energy. So, the only question then is: What are you communicating? ~ Sheli G

The Message

My husband, Terry, and I were going to be visiting Northern Idaho. Several days before our trip, we discussed that our flight left at 9:00 am and that we would leave home at 7:00 am to arrive at the airport in plenty of time. The night before, I set our alarm for 6 am so we could be ready to leave in time for our flight. At 6:50 am, I stopped by my office to quickly pick something up for the trip, and then at 6:58 am, I pulled the car up to the door so we could load it. When I walked in the house, Terry said, "I'm going to use the bathroom real quick." I hugged my son (again!), washed our coffee cups in the sink and piddled around for what I thought was just a couple of minutes. When I glanced at the clock, it was 7:15 am. How did that happen?! Where had the time gone? I walked over to the bathroom door and inquired, "Weren't we leaving at 7:00?" Terry came out right away, we quickly loaded the car, and by 7:25 am, we were on the road to the airport.

Once on the way, he asked, "Does our flight leave at 10:00?" "Our flight leaves at 9:05," I knowingly revealed our drastic situation. If we even made it on time, we were going to be cutting it real close. Somehow we made it to the airport at 8:40 am, parked, checked in, got through TSA and arrived at our gate at 9:00. Yes, sometimes God does miracles even for those who run late.

The morals of the story:
Don't assume. It never hurts to confirm what you even think you have already agreed on. A quick, "If I set the alarm for 6:00 am, that gives us enough time to be ready to leave at 7:00, right?" would have done us a lot of good.

Don't lose your cool.
I didn't get upset when I thought we might miss our flight. I took equal responsibility for not confirming what time we were leaving.

Learn from your communication mistakes.
Coming home that weekend, Terry made double sure he knew what time the flight was and wanted to be at the airport three hours early! We compromised and arrived an hour and 45 minutes early. Let's just say, arriving last minute by the skin of our teeth won't happen again.

General communication tips:
Know what you're talking about. Never try to build a case you know nothing about.

Listen more than you speak. Focus on understanding what the other person is saying.

Listen, then speak back what you understood the other person to say. "This is what I hear you saying..."

Say what you have to say, *even* when it's uncomfortable or uneasy, in a way that doesn't harm your relationship.
Some of the toughest conversations you will ever have are the hard ones. But, they can be the most rewarding in the end and build amazing bonds in your relationships. Don't ever hold back what you have to say: speak your truth.

One of the best ways to heal is simply to get everything out. When you hold in who you really are, even just a little bit, you can prevent yourself from healing. We all have a story. If there comes a time you feel you should share a piece of your past, trust yourself. Share it. Bringing your past out into the light can be a very healing, transforming experience.

Fuel for your flame:
What can you do to be a better communicator?
What is a conversation you need to have? When can you have it?

Chapter 30: Guilt
by Terilee

Let go of the guilt. We have much better things to hang onto.
~Terilee Harrison

While shame is when you feel bad about yourself as a person, guilt is what you feel when you believe you have done a bad thing, or have not done something that you should have.

I struggled with not accepting my whole self, and because I didn't like myself (or felt shame), I never shared all of who I was in my business relationships. There is a difference between shame and guilt.

Here is an example of guilt:
Many years ago, someone I know was part of an accident on the farm where they grew up. One of the results of the accident was her two-year-old brother was killed. Tragic. The accident wasn't her fault. It's still unfathomable. Yet, as you can imagine, for years she felt guilt for causing the accident.

A life-altering event like this, where you internally take on "you have done a bad thing" is *guilt*. Carrying unresolved guilt can lead you down a path where you may have great difficulty not only reaching peace, but ever achieving real success. Guilt can weigh you down like a heavy anchor.

As business owners, we have all done things we are not proud of. Here is a list of a few examples of everyday guilt:
- A client lost her house and everything she owned in a fire, and I didn't know what to say. *I feel bad now for not reaching out to her.*
- I told a little, white lie to save my employee's feelings. *I shouldn't be lying.*

- My friend on the Chamber Board needed help on the PTA Ambassador Committee, and I told her I couldn't help her. The truth is I could have created the time if I wanted to. *I feel guilty for not helping her more.*

The big, life altering guilt:
- My daughter died. Cancer swept through her and took her quickly. I was so engrossed in a project for the company, I did not get to see her before she died. *She died hating me.*
- I will never forget the accident at my shop. I should have invested in higher quality shelving to safely store our materials. One of my best employees will never walk again. Why did I cut corners? Why didn't I invest properly in my people? I was in such a hurry. *I could have prevented this.*
- The lawsuit I filed against our competitor will always weigh heavy on me. I deliberately went after them and tried to take them out of business. I was relentless and mean. I will never be able to enjoy our company's success today because I know the manner in which I achieved it. *I caused injustice.*

The Message
The power in guilt is that it's not about what you have done (or feel you should have done). The power in guilt is in what you *think.*

What causes you Level 10 pain might be a Level 3 to someone else. What do I mean by this? You and another person may have done the very same thing. Let's say you both had a disagreement with another business owner in town who meant a lot to you. But, as you both go along in your life afterward and begin to sort it out, you may not be bothered about it hardly at all and the other person might be overcome with the feeling they have done a bad thing and not be able to continue along in their business in a productive way.

Here's a thought: No amount of guilt can change the past, and no amount of worrying can change the future. Have you stuffed any guilt? We live in a stuffing culture. We tend to take the pain of our past and stuff it deep down, and we don't address it.

Guilt is to the spirit, as pain is to the body. If you feel guilt today, it will inevitably find a way to seep out somehow into your business, your life, your health, or maybe even into your bank account. The weight of guilt can crush you unless you take steps to let it go.

An amazing tool for exploring around what's in our heart and mind is journaling. There is power in getting your words from your head and your heart down on paper. Get a notebook and keep it private. Make time (even a little bit every day helps) and begin writing. Write as if you are going to throw the notebook away later. What do you feel little, everyday guilt about?

Write this beginning phrase and keep filling in the ending: "I feel guilty because... I feel guilty because..." Keep writing. You may be surprised what comes up the longer you keep writing! You might discover you have become a "professional" stuffer! When you have exhausted the list of little, everyday guilt, then ask yourself: What do I feel deep, life altering guilt about? Write the story of what happened in those incidents. Ask yourself: What is the truth in the situation? Sometimes we take on guilt for something that is just not our fault. Keep writing until you feel complete.

Fuel for your flame:
What showed up for you?
Is there something you need to forgive yourself for?

Chapter 31: Hope
by Sheli G

As long as there is still breath in you, there is hope! ~ Sheli G

May the God of hope fill you up with joy, fill you up with peace, so that your believing lives, filled with the life-giving energy of the Holy Spirit, will brim over with hope! ~ Romans 15:13

We must accept finite disappointment, but never lose infinite hope. ~ Martin Luther King, Jr.

How do you define hope? I think when we have hope, we don't need to define it. But, sometimes when people are struggling to find the hope, to find the positive in life, in a situation, or inside of themselves (which is really where it lives when it's alive), it is difficult. *It's very hard to articulate into words, but hope is something that keeps us wanting to be alive, striving and thriving.*

The Message
Hope: from Wikipedia, the free encyclopedia:
Hope is an optimistic attitude of mind based on an expectation of positive outcomes related to events and circumstances in one's life or the world at large. As a verb, its definitions include: "expect with confidence" and "to cherish a desire with anticipation." Among its opposites are dejection, hopelessness and despair.

When you read stories about people who have survived crazy accidents or circumstances, and the only thing that kept them alive was the hope that one day they would survive it, escape, rise above the circumstance, or they would see their family again, there would be a dawning of a better day, etc., *if they just hung on.*

It is so hard to explain or define in fact, that we might each define hope a little bit differently. Many people liken hope to a spark, or an internal flame, that even if it's small sometimes, or through certain hard life events that happen, there is that spark of hope that says, *keep breathing, keep going, keep doing, keep trying. Don't give up.*

Sometimes it's a physical battle that we're in.
We hold onto the hope that we can beat cancer, or come out okay from a difficult surgery, accident, or some kind of traumatic event. The body is pretty amazing and resilient in the way that it can bounce back. There are times when it seems there is very little hope in our circumstances. It's hard when people (even our family or doctors) around us are saying, "Oh, she probably won't make it through the night," or "Oh, he probably won't ever walk again or play a sport again, or he's probably going to have a traumatic brain injury and be a different person."

Oftentimes, miraculously, people come back from those kinds of scenarios, and they beat all the odds that were seemingly stacked up against them. Usually, they'll articulate in some way, that there *was* hope; hope that they would walk again. There was faith that they would beat the cancer, the illness, the disease, the circumstance, the chances.

There's a resiliency and a fighter inside of us.
We will rise up against the odds, the statistics, the rumors or the negativity, to conquer and live another day, or invent new great things from the ashes, or love again after we've been tragically heartbroken.

Sometimes we struggle to maintain hope with emotional or relational challenges.
There are difficult times in our lives where our hearts break, and articulating it is hard. Usually overcoming emotional pain is much more debilitating than overcoming physical challenges. We can't control it. It just is. We feel what we feel. *They can hijack us, or at least it can FEEL that way!*

156

Feelings are not always rational, and they certainly don't ask our permission.
Feelings come in, and sometimes they are like a great white knight, sweeping us off our feet, making us feel wonderful, exhilarated, passionate, and free. But, sometimes, feelings come in like a thief in the night, taking us to our knees with grief, sorrow, pain, devastation, betrayal, loss, or all of the above, simultaneously.

Those can be difficult times to maintain the spark, some glimmer of hope inside that my heart *can* heal eventually, even though in this moment it feels like there's no possible way I can come back from this. It feels like I might as well die just because my heart hurts so much. It's some of the greatest pain in this world. It's also where some phenomenal art, music, books, and poetry are birthed from.

Sometimes we try to find and keep alive a glimmer of hope in our finances.
If you've ever been through a difficult time with money, it can seem so scary. In the American culture, there's a lot of things you can only do with money. You need to pay your rent or your mortgage, put food on your table, not only for you, but also if you provide for someone else, e.g., a family member, or even a friend or roommate. It's a responsibility, and oftentimes that responsibility of feeding someone else is a bigger burden than feeding ourselves. It takes money to keep the power on, your phone on, to keep gas in your car. We can't get work or keep work without gas in the car. There are basic needs that take money in our culture.

Even so, we don't want to obsess or focus on money. Most of us don't necessarily want to have money be our number one priority, and yet, it's a central, primary need and resource in our culture in order to survive and certainly to thrive, to scale, grow, and pursue the dreams and the visions in our hearts and minds. It usually takes money at some point, on some level, and sometimes it takes a lot of it, particularly in business. If you've ever lost it all or really struggled just to have basic needs met, much less open a business with all the costs, money can seem or feel hopelessly challenging.

Keeping hope alive is hard when the costs of a business or vision keep adding up. From the tiniest to the biggest, these costs can really overwhelm us. And sometimes, there's nothing that seems bigger than all the *bills*. If you've ever had the joy of cranky bill collectors calling you and leaving you messages or sending certified mail, it's hard to stay optimistic.

All of that can create a restrictive feeling of fear, scarcity and smallness in a sea of debt or financial responsibility.
Holding onto hope is hard after you've been bankrupt, had a foreclosure of a home, got your car repossessed, or had the power turned off. Even though you can come back from those things — we can always come back — in the moment it feels huge.

Money can be made. It can be lost, and then the good news is: money can be made again, if we keep hope alive.
But, something as simple as the power being shut off, even though it can be turned on again, psychologically can take us to our knees, derailing our emotions and affecting us on a mental level that can really bash our hope, put a damper on our relationships, our work ethic, and make us wonder, "Do I have any reason to hope left?" Have you ever felt like that?

In those times, we get to dig and mine inside ourselves to find the hope within that things *can* turn around. We get to have faith in God - to know that *there are answers if I can just make it another day or moment or week or month, if I can just keep my spirit alive to creatively think of a way to move to another paradigm than the place that I'm in now.*

As long as there's a glimmer, as long as there's some percentage of hope left, the human spirit can be pretty resilient in finding it.

It's like the embers of an old fire that have dwindled down. If we could just blow a little fresh oxygen onto it, if we can just put a little bit of energy back to it, can we rekindle the hope inside? With that fresh wind, then it can grow, expand, and once again start to revive and heal and come alive in a bigger, bolder way.

I love those epic survivor stories – the extreme ones. You know, the ones that portray the triumph of the human spirit or body coming back from the depths of despair. Even if it was down to only splinters of hope, that person hung on to faith, however small, and then somehow, some way, harnessed that spark and triumphed over the situation, the heartbreak, or the devastation that they experienced. AWESOME!

Okay, funny story here. My husband would love to just laugh and have fun all day long if he could. He cringes when I watch movies or documentaries about survivors of crazy dramatic things. He will say, "Are you watching another one of those 'I almost died 14 times, and I was mangled, and driven over by a tractor, and chewed up by a lion, and floated 184 miles downstream, and was drowned and dead, three times, then shot, but I lived and now I am telling you all about it!' stories again?" He is very funny, and to this, by the way, I passionately answer YES!

In one of the shows I watched, there was a runner who had been running way, way far out in the desert. She took her faithful dog with her. She was an Olympic-level athlete. She slid down a very steep cliff embankment, and landed awkwardly, shattering a good part of her legs and hip, and could not walk at all. She couldn't even attempt to stand up, much less walk, and she was miles in, alone, *and no one knew where she was.*

All she had was her dog. Dogs are so smart. They have such a tenacity and will to live and to work their way out of challenging situations.

This little dog ended up, to a large degree, being her hope. She wanted to survive. She wanted to get back home to family, friends, to her life and to more dreams and aspirations. To anyone hearing this story, the situation would seem almost hopeless. It would have been a sheer miracle times a million that somebody would be able to find her way out there where no one knew even approximately where she was.

There was the tiniest mud puddle next to her that, for multiple days out there in the sun, with her horrific internal injuries and internal bleeding, became the only thing that kept her alive. She, according to most doctors, should have died. But, apparently she shouldn't have died, because with this little dog keeping her company and them both drinking a little bit out of this small muddy pool, somehow, *some way, the human body and the human spirit lived another day.*

Eventually, several days in, she realized if this dog doesn't go find and bring help back, she was not going to be found in time, especially due to her condition with her critical injuries. She had run out of waiting time. The hope that somebody would just miraculously find her had died, and hope plan B took over.

She sent her precious dog and friend away. Somehow, this dog was so intuitive and smart that he knew she was sending him off. He wasn't in such good shape either. He hadn't eaten for days, and was pretty dehydrated, tired and scared because he could sense that this situation wasn't okay. He knew it was dire, and so he went. She wondered if she would ever see him again. She thought it was possible now, that she would perish alone, broken, out in the desert sun.

Her heroic, brave dog miraculously found a couple of guys, and was able to, pretty passionately, convince these guys that something was up, and to follow him. They could tell this dog was barking and freaking out for a reason. He seemed intentional about it, like he really was trying to communicate

160

something.

Her amazing dog literally led these men back to her, and it saved her life. I think stories of hope are pretty breathtaking, *and what and where we find hope can be different for each of us in every situation.*

There have been times that people have been stranded emotionally, physically, or financially, and they cry out to God, even if they never have before. They start to think *maybe there is a higher power. Maybe something miraculous will happen here that I didn't understand before. I've tried my best. I've tried everything I know and that I can do, and now I've got to rely on the force that's bigger than me, that created the earth and has so much more power and knowledge than I have to pull me out of this,* and that becomes their new hope.

It's a very defining moment in our lives when we embrace what is bigger than us, and we do survive, and we learn and grow because of the challenges.
Coming back from those weak, debilitating moments when we find that hope (wherever and however we find it) can be such exhilaration, enlightenment and knowledge that we just couldn't have known before. You can't just read about that. *You can't just hear someone else's story and get it at a deep level.*

Once you experience it yourself, it changes you forever.
The wonderful thing about overcoming is that it gives us the ability to speak about finding hope, light and truth to others when they're going through a difficult time. Not to minimize what they're dealing with, because we hang on to our memory about how difficult it is when we were in it. Usually, rational conversations don't help when you're "in it," when you're feeling hopeless and overwhelmed, and yet, I can speak to it if I know that I know what it feels like to be financially broke, emotionally tanked, physically exhausted, having no energy left, or to physically feel amounts of pain beyond comprehension.

That's the brilliance of hanging on to the hope, knowing we will make it through the tough times. We'll make it through the challenges. *We slay those dragons that show up in life in all the different ways that they will.*

When we grasp and cling to hope, however small it may feel in the moment, we can harness it and move to the next place. Then, we can help mentor others to do the same. I believe that's why we have such a heart to serve others. We desire to use the most difficult of life's experiences and our stories in order to turn hope back around, furthering our own healing to help and serve others.

Those of us that have found hope in ourselves, in God or through family and friends, we know as we hang on, as we keep doing our best right where we are with what we've got, that miracles do happen.

Miracles happen sometimes very quickly, out of the blue, and then we come out the other side.
Holding on to hope is important. To *The Ignited Entrepreneur* it's paramount, because there are times when business is going to look like a big struggle. There are times it's not fun, and adversity, challenges and circumstances will seem to come all at once. It can seem so unfair and illogical, and we just can't see clearly enough to get through it. We can't just positive self-talk ourselves enough to figure it out.

When doors close, they're meant to close, as difficult as that can be.
As a door closes, there's hope that a window will open. There's always some purpose, something for us to be learning and mobilizing ourselves into. But, so often as chapters close, we struggle to be open to the possibility that the new thing to have hope in looks a lot different than what I imagined or expected.

New hope doesn't always come from where we thought it would

(or should). It doesn't always lead us to the future that we expected. *In fact, most oftentimes, it doesn't. It looks different.*

There are no accidents.
If you stub a toe, that's probably an accident. But, in the *bigger* picture, if you're doing the best you can, if you're doing it for the right reasons, if you're serving and *being* the difference, you will come to the next moment of purpose in your journey and create a new plan. You will create a new vision that's going to put you in the place that you should be.

We get to evolve and adapt, and even though hope can come from different places, times, and things, there is always light and hope.

There is always hope to instill into others, which is so important. And, I do believe that is part of the mantle we carry; *the beautiful burden of The Ignited Entrepreneur.*

Fuel for your flame:
Have you ever felt hopeless? What happened? What did you learn?
How can you in small or big ways, starting today, help others harness HOPE, even when it seems lost?

Chapter 32: Denial
by Terilee

*Denial is a lie you tell yourself
because you are afraid of the truth.*
~Terilee Harrison

*What you deny or ignore, you delay. What you accept and face,
you conquer. ~ Robert Tew*

*Sometimes the only thing between us and the breakthrough is being
stuck in our own denial. We can keep denying as long as we want. We
can keep denying ourselves the awesome breakthrough, too. ~ Sheli G*

**You can learn great things from your mistakes when you aren't
busy denying them.**

I have an entrepreneur friend who couldn't see she needed help
growing her business. She constantly worked long hours,
complaining about the time she spent trying to grow the
business. We were chatting at an event one day, and she started
complaining once more. The woman was standing in a room of
possible clients and she couldn't get the energy to interact with
any of them. She mentioned being up most of the night trying to
reconcile her business bank account, sending out emails to
employees, and basically doing office work when she could have
been getting rest. She said her family was falling apart. She
couldn't sleep because she was so stressed over getting new
clients, yet had no time to do so. She felt as if she were at the end
of her rope, and it was taking a physical toll, also. I asked her just
one question. Have you considered hiring a personal assistant to
help with the mundane tasks so you can spend your time more
productively? She looked at me with a blank stare for a moment,
then replied, "Oh, no. I can handle the business side, I just need
to learn to work smarter."

This young friend of mine didn't realize that sometimes hiring someone to do the menial work actually IS working smarter. There are many things that need to be done in a small business. A lot of them are mundane, boring, and downright scary, but they still need to be done. As ignited entrepreneurs, we need to recognize when it's time to bring on a team member to help us do the amazing things we are called to do. Don't hesitate to ask for help, interview, talk to your other entrepreneurial friends to find the perfect fit for your business. Don't stay in denial!

The Message

Denial is a natural coping mechanism commonly used when something happens that we really don't want to see. *Denial is the worst kind of lie, because it is a lie you tell yourself.*

Throwback to May, 1996.

I'll never forget the day I learned everything my previous husband had ever told me about himself was a lie. He had already put me through so much during our time together. I was exhausted, stressed out, and completely overwhelmed when I placed a phone call that brought truth to my utterly chaotic world. It was then I learned he was from a different country, he was older than he told me was, several people he had introduced me to as "friends" were actually his real family, *and* (to top it off) he was still married to his last wife at the same time he was married to me! I will give you a minute to let that all sink in. EVERYTHING...he...had...told...me...was...a LIE.

Had I seen the clues over the five years I was with him? Sure I had. He was an *expert* at lying and covering his tracks, using Spanish (which I vaguely understood at the time, and he never encouraged me to learn), saying he was traveling for work into Mexico (where there was no cell service at the time), and at using control and manipulation as the super glue to hold his stories together. When I would get close to being *onto* him, he would use just enough of his charm to reel me back in.

It didn't help that I had my own personal huge dose of *I'm not good enough* and *I'm getting exactly what I deserve*. I had been in denial, because I really didn't want to see the truth.

Have you ever been in denial?
Don't be in denial! Insert a "yes" here. I'm sure you have – we all have been. Although, hopefully for your sake we do not share the same "denial story!" There are five negative forms of denial we all need to be aware of, and I think in my personal case, I had a touch of them all at once.

The biggest one is denial that a problem even exists.
You think, "Well that's strange. It seems like the daily deposit has come up short, but it's not that far off." You do nothing to inquire further about the situation. Three weeks later, when the situation comes to light that your manager has been taking funds, you look over things that have transpired and ask, "Why didn't I see it?" You observed it, but you denied its connection to the real problem that existed.

Here are some other forms of denial for us to consider:

- Denial of a problem's significance. The developing alcoholic may tell himself, "Sure, I drink sometimes, but I can quit any time I want to."
- Denial that there are options available to help you. You are struggling with the demands of your growing business. You would like to hire a consultant to help you, but you believe you cannot afford it. You tell yourself, "There's no use trying," so you don't.
- Denial you have the personal ability to change. "I'm not good at accounting. I'll never be able to learn to do payroll. I can't change. I was born this way!"
- Denial about time and time urgency. You have all the time in the world, or so you think. "I don't need to get life insurance put in place now. We are young and healthy and will always be. I have all the time in the world to work on this later."

Here's a great point: You can't heal a wound if you deny it's there.

Have there been things you've tried to ignore? Focus on them. Look for the truth in those things you've been trying to avoid. Is there some truth in what people have been telling you? If so, what do you plan to do about it?

Allow yourself to feel and experience the truth. It's not pleasant to face aspects of yourself that you'd rather not see. Don't be surprised if you feel some embarrassment and depression when you first begin to make progress in confronting your denial.

You can't change what you refuse to confront.
Don't procrastinate. The longer you put off doing something about the situation you've been avoiding, the easier it is to slide back into denial. Courageously face your own behavior, make a plan to improve it, and stay with that plan through the struggle of forming new habits.

Fuel for your flame:
Where are you not being honest with yourself?
What are the thoughts or situations you've been trying to avoid because they remind you of something that you need to do?

Chapter 33: Control
by Terilee

When you surrender control, you are choosing to have hope and confidence. ~ Terilee Harrison

The key to happiness is letting each situation be what it is instead of what you think it should be. ~ Mandy Hale

Far too many people expend most of their precious, limited energy trying to control people and things, most of which they have NO control over. ~ Sheli G

I will not stress myself out about things I cannot control or change.
As an entrepreneur, there is a good type of control. But, have you ever felt the need to *over control*?

Let's look at both kinds of control. Some things absolutely need to be controlled, and it's okay. For example, you need to control your budget, your calendar, work/life balance, your priorities, and over-committing and under-delivering. It's also good to learn to say *no* to well-intentioned *time sucks*. Can you see how *not* controlling these things can cause your life and business to get off kilter?

The Message
However, have you ever felt like you needed to *be in control*? My family went through a tough year financially. In 2010, my husband had been laid off from his job, like so many others at the time. Thankfully, my business was growing, but it still wasn't enough to cover our monthly budget. I was grateful for my work and absolutely loved it, but I was working long hours, and I was tired. My husband was working part-time whenever he could find a research job, and he was also wonderful about pitching in around the house and picking up the kids from school. I kept

control of my/our schedule. Sometimes, I would wait until 2:00 pm to tell him I had a business mixer to attend that night and that I wouldn't be home until 7:30 pm. I was doing the best I could to keep up, but I was angry, I was putting a lot of pressure on myself, and it showed up as control. I certainly wasn't acting considerate or respectful at the time.

What is the difference between good control and being over-controlling? When you are over-controlling, you will go out of your way to manipulate a situation to get your own way.

What causes a person to be controlling? There are many reasons, beliefs and emotions that lead us to hold on tight and feel the need to control others, situations, circumstances, money, communications, food, workflow, details, and our environment.

At the root of it, being a control freak is a cover up for unworthiness and fear. Have you ever felt you didn't deserve support, help, or for things to go your way? Do you ever worry things won't turn out, you will get hurt, or bad things will happen?

The cost of control.
Being a control freak can have a huge negative impact on you and everyone around you, including your family, friends, and co-workers. Hanging onto control can cost you love, freedom, peace, joy, support, energy, and connection. When you try and control everything, you enjoy nothing.

Here are some ideas to help you release control:

Be honest. We all have certain controlling tendencies, especially in the most important and stressful areas of our lives. What does this cost? How does it impact you and those around you?

Be willing to let go of control. You may not know how to do it or what it would look like, but authentic willingness is always the first step in positive change. Surrendering is about choosing to trust and have faith. It is something that can free you in an extraordinary way and is all about you choosing to let go.

Do the work to recognize control. Attend experiential workshops. Include these into your budget for this coming year and every year after this. Doing your own work will help you recognize when your behavior is controlling.

These days, my family has busy schedules juggling home-schooling, ministry, and business, but we review our calendars each week and know what craziness is coming. No one needs to be blindsided about a meeting they didn't expect. I prefer support and connection to control any day!

Fuel for your flame:
Where, how, and why do you hold on tight to control in whatever way you do?
What person, thing, or situation can you begin to let go of control over today?

Chapter 34: Partnerships by Terilee

The most successful partnerships require authenticity, complete openness, and teamwork. ~ Terilee Harrison.

Just one great partnership with the right person can have an incredible impact on your business success. ~ Unknown

The Message

Partnering in business can be rewarding. It can also be extremely frustrating if you don't go into the agreement armed with the right mindset or without having all your *i*'s dotted and your *t*'s crossed. Here is some information that will help you. What should you do to get started?

Business Partnership Checklist:

_____ Decide if you are partnership material.
_____ Identify and interview different partners.
_____ Where can you find someone to partner with? *More than 70% of new business partnerships are a result of social media.*
_____ Create a partnership agreement.
_____ Choose a business name.
_____ Obtain any required licenses.
_____ Open a bank account.
_____ Set up your systems.

The key to a successful business partnership is for every single partner to "get real." Here are some ways you can get real:

Partnership requires vulnerability.

There is nothing more foundationally important that being who you really are as you begin a business partnership. For example, I am not good with details and even worse with bookkeeping. I would never want to begin a partnership claiming I had gifting in these areas. Be who you really are.

Every partnership is unique.
There are no cookie cutter partnerships. If you have been part of a partnership in the past, don't assume the next opportunity will be the same. Each partner and each company are different.

Each member of the partnership has their own story, baggage, limitations, and giftedness.

Be open to sharing your story.
Your partner deserves to know your entire story and you deserve to know theirs. Understand each other's limitations and do what you can to fill in the gap. Understand each other's strengths and draw from them. Together, two can be better than one.

In partnerships, leadership is shared. Be willing to step up anytime. Your mantra should be, "Would you like me to ___ or would you like to handle it?"

Do not ignore conflicts.
Ignoring conflicts can be the first step toward the end of a partnership. If you think someone hasn't been putting enough time in the business, or someone used funds to pay for a personal bill without asking, and you don't address it with the other party right then, things will only get worse from there. *Address any outstanding issues right away!*

Have deep and meaningful conversations.
Discuss everything. Your goals, dreams, the risks you are taking, how you think things are going, what needs to be changed. Talk about anything and everything. *It will serve your business well.*

If you are already in a business partnership, how can you be a better business partner?
<u>Give more:</u> Give of yourself freely – your connections, your

resources.

Share more: Share all you have – your ideas, your experience.

Do more: Don't get caught up in keeping track of who is doing what! "I'm doing 70% and they are doing 30%." *Just do more.*

Be more: Be all of you.

Never hold back who you are. Simultaneously, let them be who they are, too, and respect that.

Sheli G's take on partnerships:

"Expectations Conversations" are very important.

Before you even decide you are going into business with a partner(s), I would suggest you have these open-ended dialogues: What are your expectations? What are your expectations about yourself? What do you expect from your family? What do you expect from your partners? What do you expect this business to do in 1, 3, 5, and 10 years?

Of course we're speculating on the future, but this produces profound discovery about what your potential partners believe and how they react to things. If you haven't seen them go through the seasons of life, personally and professionally, you need to know what you are getting into when you sign that contract, and your partners deserve to know what they are getting into with you. As you work very closely together day after day, through the highs and the lows of entrepreneurialism, *all of your ways of being will come out to play.*

When you're interviewing someone and working on what looks like a great partnership, it's like the courting period of dating someone. We put on our best front and we edit and filter what we're saying, how we're saying it, and we show up really well in that "honeymoon" process.

But, what happens when the stuff hits the fan and life gets hard, the culture changes, and our competition moves in next door, and stresses are high, and we have major differences of opinion?

How are we going to show up then?

This relationship will affect all of the people that you are around personally, and professionally.
You're going to have business vendors that are involved with you and your partners. You're going to have employees, friends, and family who are involved, hear about it or deal with the fallout or benefits from it. So, consider all of this wisely. It's not just about the partners only. *It's also about the ripple effect of a good and a healthy partnership that is thriving and beneficial to everybody.*

People want to know that you care about their families, their causes and what beats their heart.

Whether you go into a partnership or you are a sole proprietor, no one succeeds alone. We do that in community – we do that with other people. People will sometimes betray us and jerk us around, *but people also help us and heal us, and do compensate for the areas where we are not strong.*

Nothing really successful (long term) happens without community, and it's a matter of what does that structure *look like* for me?
Do I need partners to be successful and go where I want to go, or is this something that I can start with a board of directors, mentors and advisors, and then bring on team members later? There's a lot of ways to partner with people, so I guess that's the next thing I would mention. There are less formal relationships of partnering, which I love to call collaborating or having dialogues with people, that can look like a lot of different things.

When I'm working on a project or a business, I love to "partner" with people, and we don't always write up an agreement or create a formal partnership, but we collaborate together and we work on projects. It's not always about the title. It's not always about legalese. In fact, for me at least, sometimes the legalese can start to restrict the real masterminding and the great brainstorming that the community can bring together when you're not worried about what everybody's title is.

Masterminds are powerful.
Masterminds are typically a small group of like-minded people in a group who meet once a week or once a month. They share best practices, lessons learned, ideas, and help each other brainstorm through challenges. It's a wonderful way to have a focus group where you can all benefit, and also give and serve each other. It's really a win-win for everyone involved as long as you have someone facilitating it, or you're watching the clock to make sure everybody has a chance to both give and receive. Collaboration is one of my favorite words, and I know it can seem like a trendy buzzword in this day and age.

We are creators.
We may not create the universe like God did, but we each create something every time we walk into a room, every time we speak, every time we communicate with someone, or use our body language: we are communicating. We are transmitting messages and signals out to the people around us that reverberate. Partnerships and collaborations that can give each other feedback are the best, *because Iron sharpens Iron.*

People are watching you.
They're not only watching you on your business page, but your personal page. So really, your personal page becomes your other business page. You have two business pages. In fact, you have many business pages if you are on LinkedIn, Facebook, Instagram, Twitter, Pinterest, and all the social media sites that are so popular today.

The big name social sites will probably change over time. But, how you show up in all of those modalities, people can tell if you are just taking or if you are also giving. The percentage matters, too. If you're just giving a little bit, trying to give just the very minimal amount needed so that people assume that you're an okay person, people sense that, too. But, when you give from your heart, serve people, really want to see everyone else be as successful or more successful than you, when you really care if other people's dreams and ambitions come to fruition, and you desire to play a little part in that, people can also tell that. Your employees can tell. The vendors that work with you can tell. The people in your association can tell. Your competition can tell.

It's not just about business. We are doing life.
We are doing life with the people we collaborate with. We are doing life with the people that we partner with. Why not have joy doing it? Let's laugh. Let's have a good time, and sometimes let's just be silly, relax, have FUN, and for a minute not worry about all the *to do's*. When you're like me, that can be tough.

I choose to surround myself with people that not only believe in my business and my vision, but they believe in me and my family.

It's the little things that sometimes say, "I believe in you."
And, I don't just believe in you because I want something from you, although we all have *our* dreams, which is wonderful. I believe in you because you deserve to have *your* dream as much as I do. I believe there's a miracle inside of you just waiting to be born. I believe there are strengths in you that you don't even know exist yet, and *I want to help you mine them out, find them and fine tune them to their highest capacity.*

Fuel for your flame:
Do you think you will need a partner? Why or why not?
What are your risks if you take on a partner?
If you don't want a partner, do you think collaboration is valuable? Why?

Chapter 35: Quit
by Sheli G

Quit quitting on your dreams, your unique voice, your beliefs. Sometimes it's hard, but don't ever quit on your truth. ~ Sheli G

The best way to guarantee a loss is to quit. ~ Morgan Freeman

I hated every minute of training, but I said, "Don't quit. Suffer now and live the rest of your life as a champion." ~ Muhammad Ali

Don't quit. Never give up trying to build the world you can see, even if others can't see it. Listen to your drum and your drum only. It's the one that makes the sweetest sound. ~ Simon Sinek

Calling all *Ignited Entrepreneurs*, and those who are getting Ignited: You can't quit unless you're truly supposed to quit.

You can't quit when you *feel like* quitting, because you're going to feel like quitting even when you're on the right path. In fact, you will especially when you're on the right path!

The Message
You're going to have many moments where you think *can I do this? Am I supposed to do this? Should I throw in the towel? I can do something else. I can call it.*

If quitting is the right thing to do, if it came into your life for a time to teach you a lesson, and it's supposed to pass, then it is right to quit. Many things have a natural beginning and an ending, an alpha and omega.

"If at first you don't succeed, try, try again. Then quit. There's no point in being a damn fool about it." ~ W. C. Fields

There are many things in our life, such as causes, relationships, phases, or businesses (especially for those of us who are serial entrepreneurs) where we don't immediately find that thing we're supposed to stay in forever, straightaway.

Some things are for a time and have a natural expiration date. Let it be.
Oftentimes, owning your own business leads to serial entrepreneurialism. Why? Because we learn from every venture we take on. Each one is a stepping stone and teaches us a special educational process, beyond school and beyond the books. They're the life experiential processes that equip us with different tools and strengths we'll need, so that when we find that sweet spot— our true long-term, sustainable passion, cause, or calling—we finally have the ability, the knowledge, the experience to see it through.

It's hard to see it through.
There are days that aren't pretty, in fact, some days are quite ugly. You know, those days where nothing seems to go right, and they may turn into weeks, even months. We may go through difficult economic times, cultural changes, or even changes in our own personal life that affects our business, focus, *or our very motivation.*

That experience is invaluable, not only from the successes of some of those stepping stones, but from some of the big fat failures.
I have learned as much about business from my mistakes as I have my successes.

Get beyond the emotionality of the days we want to quit. Keep going.
When you get on the right course, your intuitive self, when you dip into it, will know. It will confirm, and affirm. Your emotionality sometimes will lie to you and say, *nope. You can't do it. You're not good enough. You don't have the skills. You don't have the support. You don't have the patience.*

Emotionality is important. It's critical. It serves us. But, be careful, it can also lie, especially if it's the only thing we're listening to. Emotions, again, being only one spoke in the wheel, are not the totality of truth. It's always just a portion. It may be true that *today I feel like quitting*. It may be true that financially there are moments where you feel like *it's pointless*. It may be true that I have days where I lack clarity, but that feeling isn't the totality.

The good news is, we get to factor in our calling.
We get to go back to our *why*. Why am I doing this? Why did I begin to do this in the first place? I was really convicted at one moment. I was sold out. I was bought in. I knew that I knew that this was *it* for me, and not just for a while and not just as an experiment, but as a long-term, life purpose calling, career, or cause. *So, go back to your why when your emotionality tells you to quit.*

Go back to your *why* when your support system tells you to quit, when the people around you say, "Throw in the towel!"
When they say; "This isn't you. This isn't prosperous," or whatever the messages sound like, revisit your *why*. They usually mean well. As long as you are grounded in your *why* and your cause or career is just, sometimes we get to tune out the noise of popular culture or the people around us, even sometimes our closest friends and family. We can compassionately tune into our own voice and our intuitive self when we know we are on the right path.

Sometimes we get to tune out the noise of the economy.
The economy comes and goes, ebbs and flows, and it gets crazy. You're probably going to go through some tides and turns, unless you're independently wealthy to start with. *That is part of the territory of entrepreneurialism.*

There can be times you start something, and the economy is really good. Then, it's a surprise and a shock when you go into a downturn, your competition moves in next door, social media changes, etc., and the entire landscape of what we used to do that was sustainable and created success is gone. The rules of the game of success always change, except for some foundational fundamentals, and we have to move and evolve into a brand new state of adaptability in order to sustain success or to find success again if we go through a real downturn.

What about when you have economic upturns, and you make a bunch of money, and it almost looks easy. Great! How are you saving? How are you investing? How are you setting something aside for when the economy flips another downturn your way? It is like a card game, and sometimes you get handed a stack of cards that you didn't ask for. Maybe you are playing to win and doing everything well and right that is in your power, but there are certain things that are out of our power. *But, that doesn't necessarily mean you should quit.*

There is both the bliss and the agony of working with people.
If you have employees, they can be one of the hardest parts about owning your own business, managing a cause, or anything that involves teams. People are beautiful. They're amazing. They also have opinions. We were raised differently, so we believe different things. We do have very different strengths and ways that we look at things, ways that we view things, ways that we would handle things if it was up to us. If there were ten different people in a room, they would all call the same business a different name. They would all manage the team, if they were managing, differently.

It's important, from the top down, to use your strengths, your abilities, and your experience to discover the best and highest ways to lead people. Lead from a place of inspiration and empowerment. Lead from a place of supporting people to get what they want, not just to get what you want. Support people to constantly be learning and growing in themselves, as a person, and as an employee or a team member, because those are the people that are going to be the most successful, the most happy, *and create the most positive culture in your workplace.*

When there is high turnover, it can be a huge frustration for the business owner.
It's not easy to find good people. It's harder to keep good people, and then continue to grow, because everybody wants them. For the majority of people, the number one motivator for happy, long-term employees is actually the culture of the workplace and how much they feel respected. If they feel like their job is of value, if it creates a significant difference on some level for the organization, if they feel positive about it, most people say that's their number one reason they stay working on a team or in an environment. People need to feel loved on. *They deserve to feel appreciated.*

Good employees have to know what they're doing well, not just hear about the areas they need to improve upon.

They need to know when they've rocked it out of the park, and that they're a hero and a rock star. They need to be told those things, and they need to be lifted up. Now, some people don't like to be lifted up like that in public, so you need to understand the love languages of your employees. Some people want to be lifted up in front of everybody, and if you don't, they're going to feel really left out of that praise. Those people definitely want the credit when credit is owed to them. Too many owners, managers or team leaders will actually *take* the credit themselves for things their team members have done, when a really epic idea, a title for something, a vision or direction came from an employee or a team member. That's a quick route to bitterness.

You cannot keep great people, with great ideas, and great passion if you steal the goods; if you claim the victory they brought to the table.
You're stealing gold from yourself too, because they're worth their weight in gold for your organization. A great employee will continue to bring value, ideas, and concepts as long as we give

credit where credit is due.

Otherwise, they will quit.
There's a fascinating story about quitting or not quitting. It's a story that not everybody's comfortable with because it's about war. It is rather unfortunate that human beings, over the history of time, for a multitude of reasons, go to war. I'm not a fan of war. That's not something I think of as wonderful or support in any way. But, I do like to look at stories of history; all kinds of historical stories of real people and learn from their epic highs and their tragic lows. I learn from it; learn what did work and what didn't work in regards to what makes us successful in relationships, in business, or in our families.

This historical account is about Hernando Cortes. I find the story around what happened very interesting, and I think it proved some good points. Here's this young guy (early 30s) who decides to do something absolutely audacious. It was truly, on paper, an impossible goal. He was outnumbered 10,000 to 400. The odds against him were incredibly stacked. *Nobody would have put money on him as far as the odds go. Have you ever been that guy or gal?*

How many times in life do we *not* try something because it looks impossible, we think it's impossible, or we hear that it's impossible? Things are always impossible until they're done. Somebody runs super fast, and we think, oh! It's the fastest mile anybody's ever run. It could never happen again, until...it happens again. *Somebody comes up and has the courage, the tenacity, and the commitment to do it.*

Anyway, Cortes says I am going to go to the Yucatan Peninsula to overtake the Aztec Empire. He claims he did it in the name of Christianity. That was a common claim for conquerors of that time. It would be very interesting to interview him. We cannot do that at this point. And so, he makes this decision, and at first the Governor of Cuba is going to endorse and even financially support this voyage. As we all know, war is an incredibly expensive venture. It requires equipment, soldiers, horses, ships, weapons, etc. But, at the 11th hour, right before this expedition was going to happen, the Governor of Cuba pulled the funding and his endorsement. *I think for a lot of people, and perhaps rightly so, they would've quit at that point.*

When the business loan, crowdfunding, the rich relative, investor, or the SBA loan doesn't come through, it's a popular time to quit.
The capital to start a business or keep a business going in its formational months, or the first couple of years, can suddenly change, and the rug is seemingly pulled out from underneath our feet. Some people easily throw in the towel then. That's okay. *Sometimes it might be the right thing to do.* There may be a reason the funding did not happen – there are no accidents.

Sometimes when things fall apart though, it's possible they're not meant to happen.
Cortes didn't see it that way. He decided these new circumstances hadn't changed anything for him, but he had to change his plan. He had to process his options. *How am I going to make this happen? The way I was going to go about this just blew up. I've got to adapt. I've got to evolve, get creative, and think about this differently.*

Cortes takes a very unique approach, which I find intriguing. He put all of his own money towards this venture. He was definitely "all in" at that point. It's one thing when an investor or bank is funding your entire operation, but when you take every penny that you've ever had and you "put all your chips on red" in the gamble, going all in, that really changes the dynamics. *Would you agree, his commitment level, psychologically, financially, mentally, emotionally took a big shift at that point?*

He put it all on the line.
This voyage was going to be years of his life, not months. This was going to unfold as one battle after another battle as the years

went on. It wasn't going to be an overnight success. Truly, most successes are not, so he already knew he was going to leave everyone and everything behind. *Now he's put all of his resources IN.*

Here is another critical move: Cortes can't just hire mercenary soldiers, because he doesn't have that amount of cash. So instead, he activates what I think is a brilliant plan. He enrolls a bunch of farmers to be his army, to be his soldiers. What do we know about farmers? They are some of the most hardworking people you could ever hope to meet in your life. They literally work from sun up to sundown. They're very responsible. They don't sit around and whine, thinking about what's not working for too long. *They just get up, go out, and make it happen, day after day, year after year.*

Farmers are tough! They're tough because the job is tough, and it takes a lot of different skills to make a great farmer; skills they've learned for years in these family businesses. And, there's a tremendous amount of loyalty with those jobs. They don't just start and then quit a week later. They are in it to win it from the beginning until the end, and so their loyalty is usually second to none. I must say, a very strategic move for Cortes.

Sometimes we have to let our visionary self take a nap and let the strategic player inside of ourselves make a chess move.
He obviously had some good strategic and creative thinking skills to not just throw in the towel the minute his plan A completely blew up on him. It wasn't like it blew up months in advance, but right before he was supposed to go. He had to completely recreate the vision of the HOW he would go about his goal, and he did.

The farmers that went in, they were men of their word, but they also put their money into the expedition, too. I would've loved to have heard the sales pitch that Cortes gave the men, especially with the ridiculous odds against them! *How did he convince them to go in on this investment?*

The Aztec Empire was very rich. And of course, the big controversy about that war was did they really go in for Christianity as Cortes claimed, or did they go for the gold? Some might say that they did it for both reasons. It's not my place to judge, but those are the arguments that have gone on for years. I imagine that the potential riches might have been part of the enticement. *You go in with me, and you give me your all. You give me your life, really, for at least several years or more. You give me everything you have financially, and you stand to come out a very wealthy man at the end when we win.*

Of course, it all hinged on winning.
Oftentimes it does, doesn't it? If this works, it will be incredible. If not, I will be broke. If you lose in that kind of an arrangement, you lose everything – years of their life and time away from their friends and family. In this case, they would've lost everything that they had financially as well. And so I wonder…how did that change the game for these farmers? Instead of hired soldiers that got paid to go to war, they were paying to go to war and to potentially gain whatever they perceived they could gain.

Psychologically and mentally I wonder how being so invested prepared them. They were heavily invested at every level: emotionally, psychologically, financially, time, energy, etc.

They were committed at the highest level.
I think that raised his crazy odds from: *Gosh, this just looks impossible!* To: *Man, maybe these guys are just crazy and committed enough to have a shot at it!*

One of the first ways they won was simply arriving at the Yucatan Peninsula. Many ships filled with hundreds of men had gone before them, but had turned around before they even reached the Yucatan Peninsula's shores. Some of them turned around because of sickness. The men became sick at sea for various reasons. When you're in a closed container like a ship, if one person gets some kind of a disease and it spreads, that can certainly take down a crew. *I think that some of them, we can assume, probably turned around because of fear.*

Remember, there were 10,000 plus indigenous people in the Aztec Empire, so it was a huge undertaking. Sometimes we get right in the stream of doing something, and for example, you are in negotiations or are creating a contract, and you may feel in your intuitive self that *this isn't for me,* or this isn't the right time, or this isn't the right collaboration, or those stars either align or we pull the plug. In those moments, you really deserve to weigh out everything, and sometimes getting good counsel or mentoring in that process can be crucial. *But, for Cortes, his men were as committed as he was.*

They made it to the shore, and that was their first victory: no turning back.
I can just imagine them all on the shore, and we can only speculate what was said and what they were experiencing. Imagine a bunch of men together who have already accomplished their first goal: arriving. They were stoked and excited, and they were probably doing what men tend to do before games or at half time when they get each other really fired up – beating their chests and doing their war cries, slapping butts or whatever that looks like. Wouldn't we like to know what Cortes said to his men? Maybe something like this:

"Okay, men! Great job! We've made it here. We've arrived. We're on our way, and now we're going to burn the boats..."
I just imagine the hush that might have fallen over this crowd of fired up men as they go from celebratory and excited that they've survived this long to..."Wait, what? What did he say? Did he say to burn the boats? Because we came in quite safely on these boats. These boats are our friends at this moment in time, and they have brought our bodies, our equipment, our horses, and everything else safely to the shore. So, why in the world would we want to *burn* those assets? We spent money on those

boats, *and they're still good boats!"*

Sometimes, it's hard to let go of what was, and what worked in our past.
Cortes said, "Yeah, we are absolutely going to burn the boats, and I'll tell you why. Once they're gone we have *no back door*. We have no plan B, literally. We are here, and *we are here until we accomplish what we came here to do."* #AllIn

Sometimes we have to thank the past, learn the lessons, but move on. And, burn our boats.
Sometimes the methods, the relationships, the ideas of the past, may have served us well before, but now they're obsolete or even holding us back. Cut the cord. Get rid of the escape route. Be in the now. Cortes did just that.

He was very clear. He was very intentional.
I don't know that he ever waivered. If he did, none of the historical accounts I've read mention anything that looked like wavering or even flinching on Cortes's part. I think that was part of the reason he got people to follow him. He had a crystal clear intention from the very beginning, and he never wavered, sold out, got flaky, or flip-flopped on himself.

It was his insurance policy. He thought; "We're not going to chicken out one day and go home. We're not going to have a bad day emotionally, physically, or be fighting amongst ourselves or for whatever reason turn around and go back to our own boats and run back home. *We are here. We are doing this."*

It was an "impossible" feat that they were trying to do.
How easy would it be to get scared, discouraged, have a bad day, or a bad battle and take your toys, turn around and go home?

Sometimes it's time to be in. Realize all of those challenges and obstacles that are going to come our way are part of entrepreneurialism. They are part of any relationship or any goal

187

that we go after. It's not always going to be smooth sailing. It's not always going to look like what we thought. And so, will we just take our toys and go home even when we shouldn't, even when we know that we know our *why*?

When is it time to run and go home, and when is it time to look fear in the face and say, *yeah, I'm scared, but I'm going to continue on anyway*?
No, I don't have all the answers, but I'm going to continue to seek them until I find them. I don't have every strength, but I'm going to surround myself with people who can help me compensate for my lack of strengths. I don't have all the capital, but I'm going to look for investors willing to invest in this and help me. *I'm going to look for and attract like-minded people who catch this vision.*

I don't know what the economy's going to do. We never know what the economy is going to do, but I'm in it to win it. I'm here for a reason, and whatever obstacle comes my way, I'm going to work through it. I'm going to get around it, over it, blow it up, but I will continue on consistently, with famer-esque commitment. Cortes was all in, and so were his guys.

When you have a good, hard-working, committed, passionate team, that is a huge success key.
If you're interviewing people and they say, "Sure, I'll give this a shot," or "Sure, I'll try this," for me, that's a massive red flag. I don't hire people who say that. Why? Because they've already given themselves the chance or the option to fail and quit. They already don't know that they can do this. They're already not clear that this is the right thing for them. To start out on that premise means it's going to be difficult, if not literally impossible, to get it done. You deserve to be super sold out at the beginning and be all in and say, "I'm in it to win it, no matter what. I'm going to blow through every obstacle, *and I'm going to leave it on the floor.*"

I'm going to do everything within my power, every day that I can, as long as I'm called to this.

If we start with hesitation, back doors and a plan B, that is a very poor representation of our commitment level. I would question that there's any commitment at all, because half a commitment won't get you anywhere as an entrepreneur when you own your own business. You've got to be really sold out. *No matter how you feel, get up and put on that same tenacious commitment level and consistency level.*

Find ways to rejuvenate yourself.

Find ways to re-inspire yourself. Surround yourself with a bunch of amazing people so that you can keep on keeping on, even when the days are tough. That's one of the secrets. This is one of the ways that, in that moment, Cortes gave himself that insurance policy. They went to battle after battle, month after month, which became year after year. This was a long journey, and I think in business that's true, too. Success almost never happens as quickly as we think it should or want it to in business: getting off the ground, becoming profitable, building the dream team that we need to facilitate the vision, getting the right office space or product line, or whatever success is for you.

Those things just take time, energy, money, creativity, and reinventing things when what we originally thought doesn't work, and that was true of this story as well. Eventually, Cortes did win. I think he was so committed to this goal, no matter what, and that inspired some men to follow him, and it inspired them to do the same thing, to choose *in* at these high levels, even with great odds stacked against them.

If you read the statistics of how many businesses fail, and if you focus on that, you'll probably never start a business knowing there are a lot of people who fail.

What the statistics don't say is that most businesses that succeed have owners or managers who have been in ventures before that failed; previous ventures teaching them great lessons. They had a start and a finish, and you can call those failures, or you can call those really important stepping stones to the successful business.

But, here's one of the secrets of this story. I'm not trying to glorify what Cortes and his men did. The Aztecs were conquered, and there is a part of me that is very sad about that. I don't want any people to ever be conquered. I just find the story interesting, again, for the lessons. I think we are all here on the planet with our purpose and our calling, and everybody is precious. Everybody is valuable and should have their voice. But, one of the reasons the Aztecs were conquered had nothing to do with Cortes. It had nothing to do with his army, his tactics, his strategic planning, his commitment level, or any of those things.

Their failure or loss had everything to do with fragmentation.
By fragmentation I mean, 10,000 plus Aztecs...thousands and thousands of these strong, brilliant, beautiful people with all of their amazing cultural influences and history.

Even so, they were fragmented from tribe to tribe. They were often fighting amongst each other, killing off their own.
Even inside each tribe, they were so busy fighting each other and killing each other off that they lost. They were spending a lot of time and energy with *power plays* within their own tribes, so much so that when the enemy came, they had already fragmented their energy and their focus and their anger. They're so busy with the internal power struggles that they clearly were not prepared at the level they needed to be, or focused and intentional about fighting this enemy off. If they had been, Cortes or anybody else would've never conquered these people. It wouldn't have been possible due to their sheer number plus their strength, amazing culture, abilities, and their callings in life.

Had they bound together, they never would have seen defeat.
Had they really seen the enemy and said, "Nope, we are going to unify, even though we've had all of these inter-organizational challenges going on. We're going to see a real enemy for what a

real enemy is, and we're going to bind together and be stronger than ever before. We won't let anybody penetrate what we've got." But, unfortunately because they were so fragmented, they were at a disadvantage from the beginning. They weren't unified, and they weren't putting aside these silly battles and selfish quarrels that they had amongst themselves. Obviously, Cortes and his men were very unified. They were all one team, and they worked effectively as a team. They were very cohesive in what they were there to do, how they were going to do it and why they were doing it. All the tribes, with so many different agendas and opinions, didn't have that unification. Cortes and his men not only appeared stronger, but that psychological strength of the clarity or purpose that Cortes and his men had, it influenced a lot of the natives to join with Cortes and his men. A lot of them looked and said, "Those guys have got it goin' on. They know what they're talking about. They are proud. They are strong. They are clear. They are moving together in a unified front." And, it became attractive. It was a greater influential pull for them to join Cortes than to stay within their own tribes and defend their own country. It's easy, I guess, to judge and read the story and say, "Why? Why would they quit their own camps and join him?" Of course, if the tribe got defeated, there might not have been a choice, but some of them, from some accounts, say they willingly joined Cortes and his men.

The fragmentation, lack of focus and lack of clear intention about who they were in defending themselves and binding together in the face of adversity, worked to their disadvantage, because it created some chinks in the armor of the Aztecs. It created and exposed some weak spots. If a sports team is playing another team, they will analyze the other team, looking for where the strengths and weaknesses are. Every team has them, just like every individual has them. Sometimes it's all about strategy. You might have two teams that are really resilient and amazing, but if one team does a really good job of strategically planning and moving forward as a unified body or group, and the other team is very fragmented and has different agendas and isn't playing together well, they can be a lot more easily overturned than the team that is unified and has a gelled philosophy, vision or strategy, or all of the above. I don't think Cortes or anybody could have beaten them without those weaknesses. I think that's a great lesson.

Our teams need to be unified.
We need to know what our strategy is. We need to know what our marketing is. We need to know who we are as a company, what our product is about and what we believe. What are our core values as an organization? People need to be bought in to those. Even though we have different strengths, opinions and experience levels that we bring with us, we've got to be able to buy in to everything that a company, an organization, or our product is about on most levels to have enough unification to move us together through difficult times, keeping us cohesive and congruent. That way we're strong, and we don't look like a team that's fragmented and all over the place. We don't look and act like *20 people that work for 20 different companies.*

Our company culture needs enough synergy about who we are, what we're about, what we're doing, and why we're doing it to make us strong, consistent, and viable out in the community.
Just learning the lessons, I think, is great. In closing up this chapter on quitting, I have no judgment about whether you should do something or not. There's no pressure for everyone to become an entrepreneur. I actually don't believe that everyone is called to be one.

I don't believe everybody is called to be an entrepreneur.
I think it does take certain strengths, commitment levels and courage. I think some people can cultivate those within themselves because of their heritage and their giftings, and I think some people are better in support roles.

But, if you're really called to it, if you know what you're supposed to do, if you know you've got the strengths to do it, even though it will be hard, it will be worth it. Even though you'll have days of doubt, you will be able to overcome those as you keep moving forward. You will keep getting better at what you do.

You will be able to survive the storms because you're doing what you need to do, and you know that you know it, in the depths of your soul, and that *knowing* will make you *The Ignited Entrepreneur*.

Fuel for your flame:
Have you ever quit something before and you regretted it? What happened?
Are you confirmed on the path you are on now? With business, your cause, a project? Do you need to do more soul searching, research and get more advice from experts? When do you think it is okay to quit?

Chapter 36: Inspiration
by Sheli G

When your inspiration fades, and you begin acting out of trying to "motivate" someone or a group, you can easily move into control. Control is one of the most uninspiring, restrictive influences in the world. Control restricts. Inspiration expands. ~ Sheli G

To inspire someone is to breathe life into them, to engulf their spirit in a fire that draws them willingly. ~ Sheli G

Inspiration. One of my favorite words and roles, ever. It means to inspire. As a Keynote Speaker, Business Consultant, or Workshop Facilitator, this is usually an agreed upon or implied part of my job or expectation from my clients, if not the whole point of my being hired!

The Message
What a tough job it can be, you see, to inspire another. I feel one must be inspired themselves. In-spired comes from the words *to be in spirit*, from your spirit, or spiritual side, *which is to come from the power within.*

There are two words that are often interchanged, yet actually mean totally different things. One is *motivate*, and the other is *inspire*. Let's examine them.

If you are simply using skills, tricks and learned expertise, then I believe you are trying to motivate others, not inspire them. Motivation comes from the outside.

Here is an example: A coach is screaming at me. I run faster so he stops screaming. I'm motivated to make the noise quit, but I am not inspired or moved from the inside to run faster.

Motivation wears off.
It's an outside prompt or stimulus. Motivation won't get the vivacious, ultra-committed, and amazable results that inspiration can lead to, especially in the long run. In fact, it can be experienced as a manipulation, coercion, force, and abuse. You might know it as guilt-tripping. You get the idea. *People often feel resentful, hurt or angry when they feel like they have to do something because of pressure from outside forces versus a stirring from within.*

Motivation might be the push, but true inspiration is the pull.
Sometimes, we all need a little motivation to get something done, meet a deadline, or show up. And sometimes, our employees or teams need this too! But, the overall pull to enroll people to support a vision long term, is being internally inspired by it to really cause a committed drive.

Here's how the Online Etymology Dictionary defines *inspiration*:

(Noun) c.1300, "immediate influence of God or a god," from Old French inspiracion "inhaling, breathing in; inspiration," from Late Latin inspirationem (nominative inspiratio), noun of action from past participle stem of Latin inspirare "inspire, inflame, blow into," from "in" (see in) + spirare "to breathe" (see spirit).

Inspire
(Verb) mid-14c., enspiren, "to fill (the mind, heart, etc., with grace, etc.);" also "to prompt or induce (someone to do something)," from Old French enspirer (13c.), from Latin inspirare "inflame; blow into" (see inspiration), a loan-translation of Greek pnein in the Bible. General sense of "influence or animate with an idea or purpose."

Spirit
(Noun) mid-13c., "animating or vital principle in man and animals," from Anglo-French spirit, Old French espirit "spirit, soul" (12c., Modern French esprit) and directly from Latin spiritus "a breathing (respiration, and of the wind), breath; breath of a god," hence "inspiration; breath of life," hence "life;"

also "disposition, character; high spirit, vigor, courage; pride, arrogance," related to spirare "to breathe."

Wow, to look at these words: Inspiration, Inspire and Spirit. Compared to *motivate*, it is quite a massive context shift.

Do you want a motivational speaker or an inspirational one influencing your teams? A motivational or inspirational consultant/coach? It's not even a question once you understand the significant difference.

We are in a culture, both with work conditions and personal collaborations, where we are hungry for inspired meetings, strategies and goals. Millennials, who will make up 75% or more of the workforce within ten years, not only crave inspiration over motivation, they demand it. They won't settle for less, and they can sense the difference a mile away.

The days of old school, good ol' boy, top-down leadership are over. It's an extinct way of operating, and I promise you, if a leader is operating in this way in a corporation, small business, MLM, or non-profit, their influence and results will also soon be extinct. Brands and organizations go under while holding on to these old, worn out tactics...*like bad anchors tied down to yesterday.*

Your vision when starting any project or business, I would submit, deserves to be truly inspired!
It's what will keep you moving in spite of your moods, market conditions, and ups and downs. *It's the "glue" that can hold you tight when all else fades away.*

I've seen a lot of business ventures fail because they were motivated by someone or something into action, and it wore off.

Fuel for your flame:
What inspires you to act? Engage? Mobilize yourself? As a leader, how do you inspire others? Do you ever catch yourself trying to motivate another?

The Ignited Entrepreneur
Is Real. Really.

The Ignited Entrepreneur is not a role, a show, or a stage name. It's you; the real you with the masks down, with all your strengths and struggles. Ignited Entrepreneurs don't use "authenticity" as a tired word of rehearsed rhetoric, they bring their total selves to this game, and they play all out and all in. ~ Sheli G

Chapter 37: Unique by Terilee

Do you embrace your uniqueness or do you hide who you really are from the world? ~Terilee Harrison

You are exactly who God designed you to be – just the way you are. ~Terilee Harrison

You are given one life to live. Live it with dignity.
I see many photos on social media every day. One day, I saw a photo as I was scrolling down through my newsfeed that reminded me so much of my life, and I couldn't help but to stop and save the image.

Have you seen the Disney movie *Dumbo*? The Facebook photo contained two photos of Dumbo the elephant.

In the first photo, Dumbo's ears were wrapped up tight around his head in an effort to hide how big they were from the world. In general, elephants don't have small ears, but Dumbo's ears were gigantic. He didn't look "normal." In this picture, he was looking down, and his eyes were sad and tired.

In the second photo, Dumbo was bright eyed and looked happy. His enormous ears were free and displayed for all the world to see.

The caption said, "Own it!" The thing about "owning it," in Dumbo's case, is his ears. They were the cause of much embarrassment to him, but they were actually what made him unique, special, and extraordinary. He had a gift that others didn't have. He could fly!

I have experienced both sides of Dumbo's life. I have lived knowing I was different from everyone else and was encouraged not to let other people know (because they might make fun of me). Just like Dumbo, deep down I felt sad and tired inside. Very sad and very tired.

The Message
What makes me unique is I was born with several abnormalities, and I had three surgeries by the time I was 14 years old. I have a double kidney on the right side, I have Scoliosis (curvature of the spine) and I was also born with an underdeveloped reproductive tract (which in my case meant I was born with an under-developed vagina.)

I have what's called MRKH Syndrome, and it's what makes me identify so much with Dumbo! Dumbo was different than all the other elephants, and I took on that I was different than all other girls (bam! Life changing, earth-shattering self-belief).

We are all unique in our own way.
Sometimes our uniqueness is obvious to the world, *and other times it's not.*

I didn't own my MRKH for 30 years. I lived my life like the first photo of Dumbo – not embracing how I was made. I believed I was made different than all other girls. Because I didn't like myself, I ended up making bad decision after bad decision in my personal life and this seeped over into my business life. What I believed about myself on the inside is what I manifested on the outside, as it always does.

Today I find so much freedom in being loved for who I really am.
There is nothing like the gift only you can give yourself of being loved for who you really are. Once you are okay being you, the next question is *how vulnerable are you going to be?* Will you show the world your unique self?

Do you embrace your uniqueness or do you hide who you really are from the world? The good news is you are at choice. Your uniqueness can make you bitter or it can make you better. What will you choose?

When you bring out your strengths, your superpowers and/or your experiences and show them to the world, you may be surprised how others accept and admire you. We all struggle with being unique. We all long to be accepted – just as we are.

My wish for you:
May you live bravely so you feel loved and accepted today.

Sheli G's thoughts on the unique zone!
I have always known I was unique. Sometimes my uniqueness made me feel special, like I had a voice and a message that held timeless truths like many who have gone before me. *But, I also felt I had a unique perspective, to be a catalyst. An influencer.*

Then I started hearing the "too": Sheli, you are *too* bold, *too* tall, *too* skinny. You're *too* confident. *Too* white (I heard that one daily as a child, sometimes multiple times a day). Sheli you are *too* loud. *Too* positive. *Too* assertive. *Too* colorful (in my clothing, and

I really refute that one!).

It's true. When I was learning who I was and the best ways to *dance* with others (respecting who *they* were simultaneously), sometimes I was *too*...whatever. But, we are all not enough, or too much, *until we gather some life experience, feedback and wisdom.*

Then, we are not too much or not enough – we are just right.
Be you. Be your unique style, spirit and way of being. People are so incredible, diverse and special! *Like a fingerprint, leave your special stamp on the world with everyone you touch.*

Fuel for your flame:
What makes you unique?
What experience do you have that makes you unique?

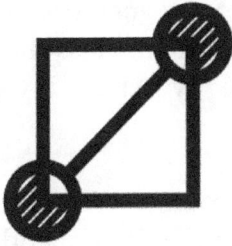

Chapter 38: Doing
by Sheli G

*What we are capable of will
blow our own minds, if we will
attempt the absurd. ~ Sheli G*

*Doing more is usually not the answer for leaders. Selfless thoughts will
change the energy by which you landscape any room you enter. Be an
artist where every soul is your canvas, and serving is your signature
brushstroke. ~ Sheli G*

Americans are great at doing. Go, go, go. Do, do, do. Unless they
have the opposite problem of doing very little due to mental
illness, bad habits, etc. Many Americans, if not most, are at
epidemic levels of *doing*. Over-scheduling, racing from one
meeting to the next, a to-do list a mile long...whew! I've found
even the retired and unemployed people I know are all crazy
busy. Hmmm.

The Message
What does this mean? Is it working? Think about not only your
life, but your family and friends too. Are they happy? Fulfilled?
Or just over-doing?

Of course we all DO have a ton of stuff that must get done.
There are things we need to accomplish. I was always good at
doing, achieving. I had to learn to focus more on the *being*.

I was 26 and had already been the top producer at a finance
company, breaking many national company records. *These
accolades and titles came at the sacrifice of my relationships.*

My next venture was to open a mortgage business, and then
expanded it to three branches in three cities. This wasn't a great
idea, as I expanded too fast in good times. When the economy
took some dramatic shifts, it was a huge challenge.

I was serendipitously invited by one of my mentors and good friend, Joni Pursell, to a personal development class that would forever change my life and the scope by which I view and experience *everything*.

It was a three month long intensive course. We were in the workshop room every weekend for about 50 hours, and we left with homework and community "pay it forward" assignments. We were all working full time, too. Yes, we were crazy. It was stretching and epic. *What we are capable of will blow our own minds if we attempt the absurd.*

Even though during those three months I was doing way more than before, for the first time in my life I learned about just *being*. Instead of focusing so much on what I had done or what I was doing, it was bringing a spotlight to my thoughts.

What were my thoughts? I started to intentionally notice. And, since everything that is created starts with a thought, it transformed my life. You see, we create something all the time. The only question, then, is: *What* am I creating? When I walk in a room, what am I causing? Does the room lift? Or, does the energy shrink or constrict. Do the people I speak to expand and open up to me with their words and body language? Or, do they shut down, and restrict emotionally. Do most people feel safe around me to share, be listened to, and be vulnerable with? *What do I create?*

Many people, including myself before this awakening, think their value is in what they do.
They don't even think about or cultivate their *being*. The truth is, if we want to produce good, ethical, compassionate, honest, dynamic results, usually it's who I *be* versus what I *do* that needs adjusting.

Thoughts become things.
If I want to do more, I'd better be passionate about it, otherwise

it's a short trip I'm on. It's not sustainable. If I'm passionate, I'm internally motivated (inspired). When I'm internally motivated, I produce more results from more energy. I create great results as I'm working in my passion, which is also something my strengths align with. I can sustain great results long term in passion, as I get refueled by it and by the results I can achieve.

This high, positive energy I create then touches those around me. They see my passion, my inspiration and commitment. Then, those who are also driven by the same passion, and those who align with my leadership, naturally come along side and produce fabulous results while being happy.

Be. The do will come. Doing more is rarely the answer for leaders and entrepreneurs wanting to expand.

Fuel for your flame:
How is your balance of DOING and BEING?
Are there things that you can cut out of the doing list, so you can focus more on creating value (habits, distractions, negative relationships, etc.)?

Chapter 39: Temptation by Terilee

A secret to overcoming temptation is to understand what you are really succumbing to. ~ Terilee Harrison

The trouble with trouble is it starts out like fun. ~ Unknown

There have been times in the months when Sheli G. and I were writing this book when I was tempted to procrastinate and delay writing my assigned chapters or when I have been tempted to avoid sitting down and doing edits. There were times when I really wanted to just spend some time with my husband, Terry, or mess around on Facebook instead. The problem with procrastination (if it happens too much for too long) is eventually you run out of time, and you can put your project in jeopardy. This is a risk I am not willing to take!

The Message

Temptation is about a wanting of something or a desire; often this is something that isn't right or good for you. Have you ever been tempted to overspend? Get into debt? Cheat on a diet plan? Have an affair? Lie on your taxes? Everyone gives into a little temptation now and then.

Part of the trouble in resisting temptation is what we desire can be forbidden or out-of-reach. Giving in to temptation can leave you feeling upset, guilty, or dissatisfied because you've done something you shouldn't have done, and you know it.

Here's the good news! You *can* deal with the things that tempt you.
Here is an example of how someone with an intolerance for gluten (but who loves pizza, pasta and bread) can deal with temptation.

What is the temptation? To eat gluten when I am gluten intolerant. I should be on a gluten-free diet. I don't get sick in a life-threatening way when I eat gluten, but I do feel tired and run down. What triggers you with your temptation? Gluten is in all kinds of delicious breads, pastas, and desserts. It's "everywhere" when I go out to eat. What are your guiding values? My values are that I love myself and want to take the best care of my body. What are you really succumbing to? When I cheat, I am taking away from my value.

Things you can do:
Exercise your willpower. I can choose a salad and decline the bread with my meal.

Plan for temptation. I can plan ahead by carrying gluten-free snacks with me so I am not starved when I arrive at a restaurant.

Replace temptation with distractions. I can begin logging down everything I eat in a fitness app to monitor my food intake.

Seek help (if needed). If things get out of hand, I can seek the help of a nutritionist.

Reward yourself. As I lose weight because I am eating healthier, I can reward myself with new clothes.

A word about the temptation to "quit" as an entrepreneur.
Have you ever met someone who switched companies every other month, or at least that is what it seemed like? Has that ever happened to you? Or, have you given your all to a business and found you suddenly lost your passion and drive for it? If this happens to you, examine this decision as a "temptation to quit!" Ask yourself, "What is triggering this temptation? Go back to your core values. Ask yourself, "What am I really succumbing to?" Make sure that it doesn't have anything to do with an underlying belief that you don't deserve success. You might be right at the cusp of greatness! You don't really want to walk

away from that, do you?

Consequences
Oops. Did you give into temptation already? You may have some consequences to pay for your actions. Be ready to accept responsibility. Learn from your mistakes. Don't repeat your mistakes. Ask yourself, "What is the lesson learned?"

If you overspend, a consequence could be not having enough money to cover your bills for the month. Now you will have to find a way to bring in more income. How can you *not* repeat this again?

If you lie on your taxes, a consequence could be you may get caught and have to pay back taxes owed and penalties on top of it. You may have to cancel your upcoming family vacation because you can no longer afford it. How can you *not* repeat this again?

Remember, your past does not define you. Don't hang onto your mistake. Let it go! We all make mistakes. *You are not your mistake.*

Fuel for your flame:
What are the things you find most tempting?
Do you need to seek help to control your desires?

Chapter 40: Grace
by Terilee

If you need a second chance today, you deserve one. Every human being on this planet deserves one!
~ Terilee Harrison

I will hold myself to a standard of grace, not perfection. ~ Unknown

Where are those black heels that look amazing with this pant suit? Why does my hair have to stick out *today* of all days? Why is there traffic *today*? I am going to be late for my speaking engagement! Oh no! I forgot to give my daughter her lunch money. Now I will have to drop it by on the way back. I feel so stressed out! How am I ever going to make it through this speaking gig?

Have you ever put pressure on yourself to be perfect? It's stressful, painful and goes against the grain of who you are. Life is much more enjoyable when you can be you and hold yourself to a standard of grace. Grace is granting mercy, kindness, forgiveness, leniency, or pardon.

Have you ever had to pay a bill and somehow missed the due date? Many companies have a grace period where you can pay after the due date before you start to incur any late fees. It's like a second chance to get your payment in.

I believe in second chances. I've been given a second chance myself. From 1991-2001, my life was a huge mess. My self-worth was plummeting. I felt unlovable. I was married to someone who was extremely controlling and always angry. I functioned at work, but was always stressed out. I was a manager and leader at work and did the best I could to stay afloat. Outside of work, I could barely keep up between his anger episodes. There came a day when things went from bad to worse, and I was able to leave him. It's what was best and safest for me and my daughter. From there, I found myself mad at men. I ended up having an affair with someone I met at work. I just wanted to feel loved. Practically all my relationships were strained, and my relationship with God was non-existent. What a mess I created!

The Message

Looking back now, it feels like the person I just described is someone else. How could that be me? Thanks to grace, a lot of personal growth, and God's help, I now love me, I'm able to love others the way they deserve, too, and I've been married to an extraordinary man for 12 years now. I've been given a fresh start, and I'm a confident business woman, thanks to grace.

I am so grateful for my second chance. If you need a second chance today, you deserve one. Every human being on this planet deserves one! We all have a story. Your story matters. It's our negative stories that can cause us to change our thinking and change our behaviors, derailing us from our path. The good news is – this is where grace comes in. Your mistakes do not define you. Owning your mistakes and taking responsibility for them is a huge step in moving forward on your journey.

It is also important to forgive yourself for not knowing what you didn't know before you learned. Sometimes you don't know what you don't know. Have you taken steps toward self-forgiveness?

Be a grace-giver.

I will never forget where I've come from. When I meet someone who is sitting in a mess they created, I know I need to extend them grace. I recall going to have my hair colored by a stressed out hairstylist I had met whose husband hadn't been working. Keep in mind, I usually manage my gray myself, so I feel like I was meant to sit in her chair that day. She needed to get her business going in a very serious way or their family wouldn't be eating. I visited with her while she colored my hair, and walked to the grocery store across the street from the shop with her and made sure her family had dinner that night.

Sometimes, people may just need a hand up, some encouragement or an acknowledgement that "I get it" and "I have been there, too." Not one of us is perfect. We don't have the right to judge others, but we do have an obligation to offer grace because it's the right thing to do.

Boundaries

I believe in second chances. I think by the time you have given someone six chances though, you should consider setting some boundaries. Some people are not safe to be around.

In talking to others, many times it's your family you need to separate from (or friends who you have come to accept as family.) You know, the ones who you have given the shirt off your back, and they just keep taking and taking. Maybe they are living with you and you find yourself working many hours to support everyone, while they stay home all day. It is frustrating, and the situation is stressing you out.

If you have someone in your life that has proven themselves unsafe, you may need to separate yourself from them. *I know that can be painful, but it can be necessary for your well-being.*

Fuel for your flame:

What grace have I received I can be grateful for?
What grace can I grant to others? Be specific, who in your life could you give some grace to?

Chapter 41: Transparency
by Sheli G

The keys to brand success are self-definition, transparency,
authenticity, and accountability. ~ Simon Mainwaring

Truth never damages a cause that is just. ~ Mahatma Gandhi

Don't fake it until you make it. BE it until you become it! ~Sheli G

I have realized that mystery is what keeps people away, and I've grown
tired of smoke and mirrors. I yearn for the clean, well-lighted place. So
let's peek behind the curtain and hail the others like us – the open-faced
sandwiches who take risks and live big and smile with all of their teeth.
These are the people I want to be around. ~ Amy Poehler, Yes Please

Transparency: another absolutely wonderful word that is really
challenging, especially for leaders.

The Message
It's not easy for the *strong*, the *brave*, or the *courageous* to be
transparent.

It's easy for us to share when it's easy.
When it's simple or when it's what people already know, it's
easy to share, be real, and be honest. It's also easy for people to
talk about transparency. It's another buzzword, a trendable thing
to claim we are. The naked leader, the open, honest, and upfront
leader is what we'd like to see ourselves as, but sometimes I
wonder if leaders really check themselves on actually living out
transparency. *It's easy for it to become pure rhetoric.*

Before I did my first personal development workshop when I
was 25, the story that I told myself, about myself was about *how*
open I was. And so, that was also the story I told others about

myself, too.

I believed I was one of the more open-minded, non-judgmental people that I knew.
That's what I told everyone. I was pretty ignorant as I look back. I can see now, it was a prideful way of thinking. It came from ego. It didn't show the humility of an open-minded, non-judgmental person. It came from a self-righteous person, who, without realizing or intending to, *I was thinking of myself better than others.* #FalseHumility

At the time, I didn't know what I didn't know.
I was so blessed to go through a three month long, incredibly intense, personal development workshop that literally changed my life. It changed the scope by which I view every single thing in my life: every relationship, function, task, goal, everything personally, professionally and spiritually. The filter changed. Who I was didn't change, but I greatly expanded. *My awareness went up exponentially.*

I can't even articulate the kind of transformation that I experienced from the inside out. It doesn't mean that I came out a perfect person, but I certainly came out understanding myself and other people so much more. That was one of the most incredible experiences I have ever had. *I'm HUGELY grateful to this day.*

The company, "Spectrum Trainings," was in Boise, Idaho. It was a non-profit that is no longer in business, but it served thousands of people at that time. What I learned was that really being open looked different than what I thought.

Being transparent means getting vulnerable, even when it's not pretty.
Transparency means being open even when it's flat out ugly and revealing of our imperfections. It's acknowledging mistakes or blind spots. We worry that if we admit them, *maybe they won't trust me as a leader. If people knew this about me, maybe they wouldn't*

think I'm the strong, courageous leader that they see when I dress up, show up, and turn on that smile. They don't see the anxiety or the stress, or the things that are not working about my business or my life, and I don't plan on letting them see.

Many claim to be transparent.
Do you consider yourself a transparent leader or business owner? What does transparency mean to you? Does that mean that I have to tell everybody everything all the time? No, absolutely not! There are certainly times and places to share certain things where it's appropriate, and where you decide who's in the room and what they need to know. You decide to share not just because of what's valuable for you to have them know, but what's valuable for them to know, or *what may not be valuable for them to hear.*

There certainly are times and places where diplomacy is king and needs to have its way.
We can be honest and polite. Here is a diplomacy example: "I read your email and I hear what you're saying, but boy, I really heard something very different in our conversation, and I want to share with you exactly what I heard, even though it sounds like we're on different pages. I want to honor our relationship and be honest, so that we can move forward."

Those are not easy conversations to have, and sometimes transparency deserves to be had face to face.
An email, text or a passive/aggressive social media post can really make things worse. #SocialTruth

When you get real and raw, do it live and in person, face to face. It's better to see the body language that goes along with the words. The greater the conversation is in depth, breadth and honestly level, the more this is true. Of course there are times where somebody is in another city or another country, and a Skype conversation or a phone call is the only option.

We get so used to our smart devices and sending messages.

#Don'tTextIt

Sending a text or an email is fast and easy, but how is that email, text message or private message being received? What are they reading into it? They may be reading it perfectly, especially if you're really gifted at words, emoticons and using a lot of different things to try to convey the emotion by which you're delivering this message. Or, they can totally misunderstand. Sometimes organizations or leaders will send out mass emails with big, difficult news, which is hard to receive in that way. Sometimes a live meeting or conference call would be better.

If there is stress and anxiety, the team feels it.

Teams know something is going on, and usually people will fill in the blanks for themselves when they don't have all the details. Of course what they fill the blanks in with is probably worse when they don't know, so be sure to be honest about the real story. You don't always have to give every detail. You don't necessarily have to give every name involved, the entire chronological order or a humongous back story, but sometimes people just need the bottom line. They need a summary or the Cliff Notes of what's going on, where we are on the road map of this business or this venture, and the direction we're still going in. That way people can bind together, mastermind, and not be sitting around gossiping and having destructive side conversations, trying to figure out what's really going on... *because nobody is telling us.*

Choose your venue carefully.

I had a difficult conversation with one of my mentors who decided he did not agree with a decision I had made. He called and asked me to meet him at a Chinese restaurant. He didn't tell me why we were meeting. I actually had no clue whatsoever that we were about to have a very intense conversation, and one where I would be on the "hot seat," one where I would feel like I got my face peeled off in public. I was very emotional, I was crying, I really didn't respond, as there wasn't an appropriate way to respond in that space.

Instead of being in the comfort of his private office, we were in the middle of the busy Chinese restaurant at lunch time! He was, in fact, very transparent, open and honest. I never thought he was *wrong* in what he said or how he said it. But, the *where* was wrong. The venue was not a successful set up. It made me feel very vulnerable. It was very awkward, and I felt totally ambushed. He didn't tell me we were going to have a really difficult conversation that I would probably feel a lot of discomfort in. Had he at least been upfront with me about the context of the meeting, I might have had an opportunity to suggest, *hey, maybe we should meet at your private office or somewhere else besides a very busy restaurant at lunchtime.*

Being crystal clear about where you're going, who you're meeting with, what personality you are dealing with, what the nature of your relationship is, and how these factors all potentially could affect that meeting is wise. Consider these before you go into full-blown transparency mode.

To create a win-win-win all the way around, you really need to consider everybody's motivation with a "masks down" meeting, and not just your own.
Transparency and honesty are things that are valuable and important when it's the right time, place, right person, and when the message is delivered in a *language and a way that the person can actually hear it.*

Sometimes, we sit around and we think about things for weeks, months or even years. We process…and we think…and we take in data…and we consider…and then we call somebody and say, "I'd really like to meet with you and talk." And, if this person has no idea what's going on, they've had no time to process, no time to think about it, collect their data or ponder how they feel or think, or what their suggestions might be about this particular thing, it can definitely create an *ambushed* perception for the other person.

You can walk in so prepared that you're not even realizing how

unprepared the other person is.

Think about the kind of languaging that enrolls, the kind of languaging that is inviting. Then, understand that they may need some time after the meeting is over, to process the information.

If someone hasn't had time to think and be able to respond right away, you might say, "I wanted to give you these things to think and talk about. And, if you open a dialog about some solutions or thoughts that you have right now, that would be awesome. Or if you like, maybe we could make a second appointment a couple of days from now, if you'd like to consider it and if you'd like to think about your perspective on these things."

Whether you agree with people or not, thanking them and honoring them for their input is what an ignited leader or entrepreneur does.
You don't need to agree to be respectful of people's opinions and their thoughts. You don't need to agree to honor the fact that they took a risk by being honest, which is sometimes difficult. *It's easy to worry about your popularity waning from being vulnerable and open.*

Sometimes you worry about what the repercussion directly or indirectly is going to be if you really tell the truth. And sometimes, I know for myself, I've been the only one on a team telling the truth, while everybody else is talking about it in the break room behind the leadership's back. That's not healthy. In order for a team to feel safe and like they have permission to go to leadership, there have to be safe places and meetings or an open door of some kind.

Create a culture where they know they can tell the truth, compassionately.
Then listen. Weigh it out and consider it before you just toss it to the side. If you open up the space and act like people are safe and they share, and then you make them wrong for what they shared, it can be devastating to people. Not only do they realize you really don't want honesty, they realize you only want to

hear what you want to hear.

Some leaders seem to want everybody to act like this admiration club and go, "Yeah leader! That's great, that's amazing, rah rah..." and cheerlead them on. But, guess what? People don't agree all the time. In fact, *most of the time, we all have different opinions about most things.*

At the very end of a delicate meeting, you might be able to say, "Why don't we meet again tomorrow and I would like to respond, if it's okay with you guys, to sum up what you said. I would like to take some time to really consider, think about it and take in your responses. Because I really appreciate your time and your honesty, I want to honor the feedback. I want to consider it carefully before I respond.

Don't say, "We're going to be transparent around here, we're going to be open and we're going to sit down and we're going to have a team meeting and we're all going to speak into this..." especially if you really don't want to hear what your people have to say. That's going to be more frustrating to them, than if you never asked.

If you want people to stay long-term at your company or on your team, create great, safe places for them to give feedback on a regular basis.
Quarterly dialogue forums can work well, or monthly, depending on your industry. Some people want to give feedback always, on all things. That is not realistic. But, setting up meetings often enough that they get to voice their thoughts (without it being a constant thing that can in fact slow down real progress) is a good mid-way solution to both needs at play.

If we all shared everything we think, we wouldn't get anything done.
One-on-one or in group settings, where people can have a voice and can act as an internal focus group, bringing their ideas and

opinions to the table, is stimulating. *Most of the world's great ideas did not come from one person alone.*

The *what's next* of leadership, the *what's next* of *The Ignited Entrepreneur* gets to really understand that this next generation coming up behind us want to be heard. If they're at a company or on a team where they're not heard, it's very much a short term proposition and they're going to leave.

What we call the *Millennial Generation*, those anywhere from 16 on up to 35, depending on which version of "Millennial" that you look at, will take up over 75 percent of the job marketplace in the next ten years.

They love and LIVE to collaborate. #LoveThem
They love to use their voices. They're very smart, internet savvy, and they love to create and cross-train. They like to speak into several different things, so they get experience and viewpoints that are a broad scope. They are intentional about advancing their resumes.

Most of all, Millennials want to create significance, both at home and at work.
They will work at places where they feel like their contribution matters and makes a difference. Where the leaders understand their individuality. Where they're able to get in spaces and places where the leadership realizes that everything and everyone is connected, and that what we all do affects one another.

Everyone works well under this context, but that's what the generation coming up behind my generation expects. And, I think they're right on the money. They're going to be the next set of leaders that teaches us a lot about how it should be done. This old 70s, 80s, 90s corporate mentality of top down, dictating to people, *and trying to control people is not inspiring, it's constricting.*

When I'm working with people, I discuss and teach on what's an *expansive* conversation (work culture or philosophy) versus a *restrictive* one?

Micro-managing people shuts people down and makes them feel restricted like a prisoner. It's a short term model. They're not going to be happy, and they're not going to produce their best results for themselves or for you. However, empowering people and inspiring them to find their own motivation from the inside out, to find their own ideas, their own greatness, and their own significance works well. Those are the people who will scale for themselves, and *they're going to scale for you, too.*

I think transparency and vulnerability go hand in hand. Let me share with you the day that changed the way I view vulnerability and its role in leadership, forever.

The Pole
My first experiential training was every other weekend for three months. We were in the room for about 50 hours each weekend, doing all kinds of interesting processes with each other. I had a team of 30 people and 10 staff.

Some of the processes seemed silly, and some were incredibly dynamic.
The facilitators put you in scenarios, and you did the process to the best of your ability, working on being open and honest the entire time to get the maximum results. *Then you noticed.*

That was a big part of it, just noticing how I showed up in those processes, noticing my thinking patterns, what I was saying, what I was doing, and noticing what was working about that (*or not working*).

The processes were micro examples of how I show up in my life everyday.
We like to say, in personal development, how you come in and how you show up in those four walls is a sample of how you're

showing up in life. If you walk into that room and you lie, then you're lying in your life, too. If you walk in and you put on masks, trying to sound better or look better, and you're not being really real and getting open, then you probably do that in your life. If you're always making excuses and you're defensive, you're doing that in your life.

It truly produced profound discovery and transformation for me.
I learned so much and really enjoyed it. It was difficult, but I noticed there were a lot of other people who also had difficulty with it. At that time, I was young and I was raised in a pretty safe bubble growing up. I just didn't have any stories like they did; dramatic and difficult life stories. At that time in my life, I hadn't really been through anything very challenging: no trauma, abuse, or addictions. So, I did a lot of watching, listening and doing my own work, but it just seemed like it was on a smaller scale for me.

On the ropes.
Beautiful McCall, Idaho, has amazing trees, a beautiful blue lake, and wonderful people. It's a small resort town, very enchanting and magical. We were out in the middle of the woods where there really wasn't anything or anyone around except for us and the facilitator who was leading a ropes course.

The course was a combination of high and low events, using ropes and harnesses.
What I learned very quickly that day was that I was absolutely terrified of heights. I will tend to just rise up to leadership roles, especially if leadership doesn't exist, or if there's poor leadership. But, that day *I suddenly felt very weak and small.*

I was the weakest link on the team.
I thought crying was weak. I don't even really know where I started to think that way or operate that way, but I liked being *strong*. I liked being the leader. I felt like people looked up to me. I thought people needed me to be strong. I didn't realize that I

had taken on that mantle. I'm supposed to be helping everybody else. I'm not supposed to be weak, and crying is a sign of weakness. I grew up in a family where my sister and I were really different, especially when we were younger. She was very relational and loving, and I remember it seemed like she cried often. She was a lot more comfortable demonstrating emotion. We're innately very different. At some point, I swung the pendulum and took on a different role. Oftentimes, if one role is taken in a family, child psychology has shown that a child will look for a different role to fulfill. No one wants to be *exactly* like their sibling. I think that was part of it, but I think I also received a payoff with my role.

There was a payoff to being that "strong" leader.
There was a payoff to starting the cheerleading squad at my school. There was a payoff to being the editor of the school newspaper or the captain of the volleyball team. There were kudos and props, and I liked that feeling. Especially in our culture, which tends to be very extrovert-driven. Extroverts often get the accolades, the kudos, the best jobs, or the best positions on the sports team, or they get elected into office or become the CEO. So, I started to learn that day on the ropes course what it was like to be the vulnerable one, to be the weak one, to be the one everyone was turning around and looking at because of the big tears in my eyes. I just didn't know where all this emotion was coming from, *but it was definitely a new thing for me.*

The last event of the day was the POLE. #OminousMusicHere
It was a massively tall wooden pole that shot up about 40 or 50 feet above the ground. There was a little bit of give to the pole. It certainly went into the ground deep enough that it was safe, but it had just a little bit of sway to it. We were to walk up the rings that were embedded into this telephone pole. At the top, you were supposed to jump off, leaping towards a large, gold ring.

I was out of my mind with fear. As I climbed up the pole, I felt okay as long as I had something to hang onto. It was when I got to the top, and had one foot on top of the pole, and I still had one foot down below on the rings, that *I just froze.*

I literally was paralyzed in that moment. I could not move my body, no matter what I tried.
I'm a pretty willful, determined person, but nothing I had done in my past worked for me at that moment. My body was not responding. My mind was trying to tell it, *move! Stand up! Do this! Oh my goodness, everybody's looking at you. This is so embarrassing. You're not this person. You're not this weak, paralyzed person...* but in that moment I truly was.

I remember the facilitator encouraging me and coaching me. "Okay, Sheli! Come on! Are we going to go?" And, I would say, "Yep. Yep, I'm going to go. I'm going!" And my words were coming out, but my body was still not moving. I could not get my body, my words, and my mind in alignment. I was staring straight ahead, and every time he would bark out, "Okay, Sheli! Now! Let's go! Let's do this!" I would hear myself say, "Yep, I'm going. I'm in!" *But, nothing happened.*

Finally, he said, "Sheli, I'm going to count to three, and you're going to sit down or stand up on that pole. One!" And, my body just shot up there on top of that pole. Boom! I was up, both feet on top, standing straight in the air with my hands out, and it was exhilarating.

Success. #BreakThrough
It feels so great when we conquer those moments of fear, doesn't it? As I was lowered to the ground, normally the large team of 30 were busy harnessing new people up, taking people out of harnesses who had gone, and doing multiple things at one time to try to keep the process moving. But, I noticed that everybody came and stood around me instead, waiting for me to come down, and I noticed that it felt really odd.

I started thinking to myself, *why aren't they all getting ready? Why are they all looking at me? This is weird, and this feels really strange.* They were all just staring at me. I had done lots of leadership things, and I had done lots of things on the stage, but it was the way they were looking at me that was really different that day.

Why are they looking at me like that?
I was excited. I had done it. I conquered it, and I was glad it was over. As they were taking me out of the harness, I looked up. Tears were streaming down my cheeks. I looked up and tears were streaming down the cheeks of all my teammates. They were looking at me with the most loving, compassionate, connected look that I had ever seen anybody look at me, other than my closest family. It was a transformational moment.

I mean this with everything in me when I say that moment changed my life forever.
That moment changed the way I do relationships, the way I do business. That moment changed the way that I will approach my calling on this planet for the rest of my life. I realized that I had been really vulnerable.

In that vulnerability, I was open. I needed my team.
They were all watching and waiting for me, and nobody was doing anything else. I was unguarded, and so approachable. It connected us on a level that you cannot articulate in words. It connected us on a level where they knew I needed them, and I did. I could never be the same. *I need people.*

I can't get where I'm going personally, professionally, spiritually, financially, or any other way without the help and support of people.
I need people, and people need me. They need what I have to bring to help them get to those places, because they can't do it alone either. That day, it took vulnerability. It took risk. It took moving through my fear, *and it took just being transparent at that gut level for that kind of connection to happen.*

You can't make that up.
You can't fake that kind of connectivity and vulnerability. And, in that moment, I realized that if we want to be amazing leaders in our homes, in our businesses, or in our lives, the secret weapon is *vulnerability*.

It's the magic formula.
Vulnerability is the potion that will create you, along with your strengths and the influential skills that many of you have because you're leaders. I know you're leaders, because that's why you're reading this book, and I do know that everybody leads in their own style, in their own way, with their own strengths.

Speaking to the leader in you, I'll say this. Leadership is not just about strength as we know *strength*. It's not just about loud or bold courage. It's not just about bucking up and shouting out that battle cry with your silver gleaming sword in the air.

It doesn't always look sexy. It doesn't always look put together. It doesn't always have all the answers. It doesn't always knock everything out of the park and create the home runs. Sometimes it looks emotional. Sometimes it looks like, *I don't have all the answers, I'm struggling, or I do not know what to do.* Sometimes it looks like, *I'm scared.*

But in any case, vulnerability says to the people around you, *I need you.* You're important. You are valuable, and I cannot do this without you. Vulnerability is the power that alongside of strength, courage, experience, and charisma creates the kind of influence that is the *what's next* of leadership. It is the *what's next* of *The Ignited Entrepreneur*.

Fuel for your flame:
How do you feel about being transparent? Do you think you are?
What do you think a leader should be transparent about?
What is Transparency to you? Your definition?

Chapter 42: Mentors
by Sheli G

We are all teacher and student, simultaneously. ~ Sheli G

Sometimes the breakthrough happens when our deepest intuitiveness combines with our life experiences to become the touchstones of transformation. ~ Sheli G

The task of leadership is not to put greatness into people, but to elicit it, for the greatness is there already. ~ John Bucha

Mentors come from many different places in our lives.
Some of our natural mentors might be parents, older siblings, aunts, uncles, or grandparents. They might have been family, friends or associates. They can be coaches, teachers or club leaders. Counselors, pastors, doctors. *Sometimes we don't even realize how powerfully someone has influenced our lives until we look backward and realize we've been mentored.*

Some people avoid being mentored.
Maybe we can eventually learn much of what we should know just by being alive for a long time. But, mentors bring that objective teaching quicker, more effectively, and help us to scale to where we want to go in record time with fewer tragedies along the way!

The Message
A great influence and foundational mentor for me was my dad. He was an entrepreneur, humanitarian and teacher. He was an inspirational and educational speaker and leader. He worked with the government in missile research before going out on his own to sell insurance. He went on to do financial planning and invest in many things from real estate, to restaurants, to gold. He had many great successes, and also had some disappointments along the way. Usually those came in the form of trusting the

wrong people, and being too idealistic in his approach. The visionary in me has had the opportunity of seeing some lessons in my father's wins *and* in his challenges.

When I started my first business at age 26, my biggest failure in that whole journey was not enlisting mentors soon enough. I did have a few towards the last quarter of the game, so-to-speak, but I would have had more success if I had them throughout the entire game (or at least halftime!).

Mentors are so paramount, that one of mine even saved my marriage.
I was referred to this marriage mentor, and he came highly recommended. Dr. Garcy had been a pastor for a long time, then went back to school for his PhD in Psychology. All that real-world experience he had was a huge asset for him. I remember him telling me that the first eight years of his own marriage were pretty tough. I was struggling with being a newlywed to a handsome guy we will call Steve (and that really is his name).

Steve was divorced, had a very ADHD, O.D.D. son who didn't sleep well at night...and to top it off, Steve didn't know how to communicate with me at all through this culture shock I was experiencing.

My emotional self and my inner dialogue sounded something like, "Screw it, this is so not what I signed up for..." and at one point, I had one foot out the door. My spiritual self told me to think about it, pray, and get counsel. *Thank goodness for my spiritual self!*

I remember this wise, elderly counselor asking me what I wanted. He listened carefully, and without any judgement. Then, Dr. Garcy smiled at me and said with authentic joy and hope, "Well let's make that happen for you!" He said that simple phrase with grounded, confident positivity that kept a candle of hope lit deep within my soul. I believed I was no longer alone that day in fighting this personal battle. And, in fact, I was not. I had a kind, educated, experienced, authentic, spiritual guide who had been in a similar place before, and he knew that he knew that he knew...something that I did not yet know. He knew my marriage could last, and he was right. I shudder to think, without Dr. Gerald Garcy in my life back then, what might have happened.

Divinely, the opportunity came, because I reached out in my need, and I showed up with an open heart.
You may be able to find the finest, wisest and most profound teachers in the world, but you still have to set it up, and show up to collect their golden feedback. You also have to be open and coachable to receive the feedback. Your amazing mentor will only work out if you do! And, as with all 360 degree feedback, *you won't always like what they say or ask.*

Those are the best teachers: The objective seers and truth speakers.

They are not there to pump your ego. #Ouch
They are there to point out your blinders, to reveal mysteries you do not yet understand, to think clearly when you cannot, or just to give you a second opinion.

Not everyone is willing to be a mentor. Maybe it's a timing thing, or they do not feel they would be compatible with you. Or, sometimes they are struggling with too many of their own demons to help another. And, if that is the case, be grateful when someone turns you down for a mentoring role. It wasn't meant to be.

When I was first called to do some of my favorite work — transformational, experiential (participants are hands on) workshops — I was very good friends with someone who was an amazing facilitator. At that time, because we were very close, because I was called so clearly into this work, and because she was one of the best...in my mind it was a perfect fit for her to mentor me! But, when I asked her, a strange silence fell over our conversation, and a little while later the subject was changed.

I was stunned, and hurt. I can only speculate why she both didn't want to mentor me, and why she didn't even reply to the request. Now I realize there are valid reasons. There always are. Perhaps she was protecting some of her styles and professional secrets, or another more personal reason like time or energy. But, I always say *hesitation is a no vote*, at least in a situation like that.

If a mentor is not clear, called, ready and excited to speak into your life, it's either not the right teacher or it's not the best timing.
In any case, trust the process. There are no accidents. Be careful who you let speak into your life. Not all "teachers," leaders and mentors are healthy, grounded, experienced, successful, or doctrinally sound. Don't just allow a mentor to *self-appoint* themselves into your life either! There is a lot of power in the world, both light and dark. The challenge is knowing intuitively and from your diligent research who your best, honest and capable mentors are. If you really tune in to your spiritual self, and do your homework, you will know. Powerful teachers, mentors and leaders get their power from one of two places: dark, narcissistic, self-gratifying energy, or holy, pure, loving, Godly places.

Pay attention. Never sell out or compromise your beliefs, intuition or safety on any level.

Mentors are not gurus.
I know this might be used at times as a term of endearment or affection. But truly, when you become a raving fan, and then it becomes almost an obsession, when you start to feel like you need to listen to this person's recordings, read all their books or go to their classes *in order to have any breakthroughs or to get an emotional high*...we have to ask ourselves if we are really being empowered. In that case, if I believe that I'll only get my power

in a room, with certain teachers, it's possibly red-flag time. Here is my concern for people who go from supportive, to fans, to cultish followers: *they often give their power away.*

I saw this in my mid-20s. I was in the early stages of my intensive personal development growth work as an adult. This amazing phase of my life was certainly filled with charismatic, intelligent, dynamic facilitators. I saw every level of admiration for them. The students were positive about their experience. Then there were the students who went to the next level and worked to be seen, heard and recognized by these teachers. They wanted to volunteer and staff for these leaders, serve them, sit at their feet and learn from them. I did some of this in my early stages of this personal growth work too. It was an amazing time of learning and growth while serving not only the teachers, but serving the students also. It was all incredibly valuable, humbling, enlightening, and inspiring.

Then there were the zealots.
These were often the ones who were pining away for attention from the facilitators, even crumbs of attention. They had that dreamy look on their face, even when nothing particularly profound or ingenious was happening or being said. They treated these facilitators like they were gods...really, waiting on them hand and foot. These followers seemed desperate to be loved, and to have these "gurus" see them, touch them, validate them, and speak intuitive truths into them. They seemed to trust these "guru-delivered truths" above all else. *From my vantage point, they gave these mentors their power.*

I've thought about this a lot. I am now one of those facilitators, teachers, and coaches. Because I am called to this, and I've studied for years, and worked very hard at this purpose-filled profession, I am very good at it. With thousands of hours and decades of experience, combined with proven positive results, I would say I'm at the mastery level in what I do. *But, I'm no guru.*

YOU have the power to take on your life and have your own breakthroughs.
As amazing as teachers, mentors and leaders are, they are not more amazing than you. Really! Get the training, education, certifications, coaching, mentoring. But, know that some of your greatest breakthroughs will simply come from time and learning only what you can experience. *Experiential learning, hands-on learning from just your own life, and watching others succeed and fail, will be your best teachers.*

No matter how phenomenal a mentor or teacher might be, never fall into the trap of thinking that you always need the next book, teacher, class or whatever to have an epiphany or an 'ah-ha' moment. Sometimes that may be true, but as we get our experience and do our work, we will also have those moments of great breakthroughs all on our own. Moments where the dots that seemed random before, now all connect together seamlessly. Moments where the thing that made no sense before, suddenly becomes the code that you crack wide open when you least expect it. Sometimes the greatest sermon we will ever hear happens on a lonely hillside, in our car driving down the freeway in miles of maniac traffic, or it's that still small voice in the night, in the dark, when the earth and we are still long enough to hear.

You don't always have to have someone or something else to be the catalyst for your breakthrough.
Sometimes the breakthrough happens when our deepest intuitiveness combines with our life experiences to become the touchstones of transformation.

Fuel for Your Flame:
Who were your mentors growing up? Who are they now?
What areas do you need more mentoring: entrepreneurship, finances, spiritual, relational?
When will you reach out to a mentor or coach that you know you need? Set a specific name and date and tell a friend to help hold you accountable.

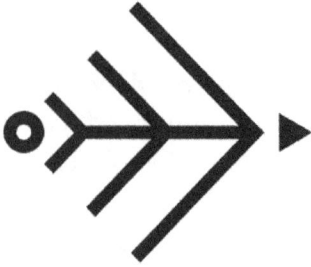

Chapter 43: Experience
by Sheli G

There are no shortcuts to experience.
Don't call yourself a master of something
without a ton of it. Otherwise, your
clients will know. ~ Sheli G

Your experiences, both the blissful and the agonizing ones, will refine
you into the World-Class leader that others will want to follow,
naturally. ~ Sheli G

No matter how good you (think you) are, nothing replaces experience. In my early 20s I learned this lesson, or at least began to. I had all the confidence, some great training, and good intuition at that age...but I lacked experience. Back then, five minutes was enough experience! But of course, to master anything, it's been said that the law of 10,000 hours of doing something is a great benchmark that indicates you are really now a seasoned pro.

The Message
Experience shows up, when you lack it, and when you have an abundance of it. I remember a time that my lack of experience, and lack of developed discernment, almost got my head knocked off.

It was early in my management career at a large nationwide finance company. I had a lot of confidence in what I had achieved there in a few short years, including being the number one loan officer in the district, breaking company records in all categories and so on. I had some experience, but I probably had more ego combined with naïveté...I didn't know what I didn't know!

I had many principles and beliefs which are good...when they are balanced out with common sense and experience. I approved a

Latino gentlemen for a loan from us, even though he had no credit at all. We called people with no credit *ghosts*. There was no real measurement or proof of their capacity or commitment to pay. *I took a risk.*

The customer came back in a couple of weeks later wanting more money, when he had not even made his first payment. In lending, this is a huge no-can-do scenario. Most banks would not have loaned to this guy in the first place. With more experience, I may not have either! But, no one in their right mind would lend our ghost *more*, when no payment had been made. I told him to pay consistently for six months and we would consider it. That was the standard answer to anyone in a similar situation.

He called me a racist, implying that because he was Hispanic, I would not lend him more money. Not only was this completely false, it angered me to my core, because I am so against racism...from anyone to anyone! I would call this situation *reverse racism*, in that I was treating him exactly how I would treat anyone in his position with credit, but because he was Hispanic versus White, he could claim that it was *why* I didn't loan him more. He screamed at me, swore at me, and as he left, he slammed our door so hard, the building shook, almost breaking the glass insert on the door.

Well...the (semi-crazy) Hulk inside of Sheli G came out. I rushed out after him. In the parking lot, I began yelling at him that he would not treat us that way. I shouted that he could go down the street to another financial institution, and get a loan from them to pay me off. I was so angry, I was almost in his face. He was, of course, screaming at me, calling me every name...

Meanwhile, my adorable receptionist Kathy was inside freaking out, ready to dial 911! She was sure I was going to get hammered. God somehow saved my face that day. I backed off, I went back inside and realized, that my decision had not been the best move on my part.

Just because you're passionate, does not mean you're prepared.
A master of something has three things: 1. talent – the raw ability some would say you are born with, 2. skill – learned from education and mentoring, and 3. experience. Experience is time spent practicing, tweaking and refining that talent, intuition and skill into mastery levels. I was a novice at conflict resolution when I took on that angry customer. *I'm lucky it didn't backfire.*

I want to share another example of what experience means in my current career, which is my true calling. That calling is about helping others find their purpose or calling in life, and finding the tools and inspiration to blow through every obstacle that will come up to block them.

One of my very favorite methods assisting dynamic human development and transformation is facilitating experiential workshops. These processes are hands-on, where the participant experiences themselves inside a micro example of how they actually show up in the macro, outside of the room.

Some of these processes can be quite challenging. I find in leading these for over fifteen years now, that people who struggle with control issues, have the most difficult time taking instructions or feedback, and basically surrendering in that moment.

Sometimes, this conscious or subconscious *need* or habit to try to control themselves, others, and outcomes will manifest in what appear to be confrontations, or "stand-offs" with me in the room. The participant often becomes seemingly childlike in their rebellious, *you can't make me* style of behavior.

As a facilitator, I can either take offense to this and make it personal, which can end up distracting the whole group by feeding into the situation negatively or with too much attention...or I can take this for what I believe it is – a teaching moment. It's a moment where what they are doing is not working very well for them, it doesn't create value for others, and it is a clear indicator of unhealthy ways they deal with this type of situation outside of the room. It's interesting to note that the rare ones (in my experience) who demonstrate this big push-back in the room, usually call themselves leaders, managers, mentors and coaches. They consider themselves to be the ones usually bringing the most value. In reality, it's true only as long as *they* call the shots, especially if they feel under fire. They tend to exhibit the *fight or flight* choices.

Experience tells me several things about these situations and the participants behind them. It's not about me. I do not ask people to do anything morally, ethically or otherwise wrong. Challenging? Yes. Honest? Yes. When I am leading in what I know I am called to do, and what I have mastered, I trust myself at every moment. Even when these tough things happen, I stay unhooked from the participant, who is trying to make it personal. I focus on not letting it derail the group, but when I discern that the participant is open, I use that teaching moment to work with the one struggling, and that helps the whole group. Sometimes we learn a great deal when we are not the ones on the hot seat, and we're just observing. Our defenses are down, so everyone wins. Experience has shown me that it's all a part of the process for those who are willing to grow.

Fuel for your flame:
What experience has prepared me for my next big venture?
What kind of experience might I still need to prepare myself for what's next?

Chapter 44: Authenticity by Terilee

The real you is the best you.
~ Terilee Harrison

Always be a first rate version of yourself, not a second rate version of someone else. ~ Judy Garland

Authenticity can be felt – in a conversation, in a negotiation, from the stage. It is obvious when someone is being themselves, or when they are trying too hard to be something or someone else. ~ Sheli G

Will the real you please show up?
Accepting your uniqueness and living authentically go hand in hand. You can't have one without the other. Once you become comfortable in your own skin, then you can step out in the world as your real self. If you have not owned your uniqueness, there will always be something "off."

People do business with those they know, like, and trust. If that's true, then why do we tend to put on a *perfect mask* to do business? Have you ever felt pressure to create a facade thinking you need to be perfect or people won't want to hire you? It's a lot of pressure to have to dress just right, have amazing business cards, drive a nice car, be positive when you're having a down day, and know all the right things to say, isn't it?

Many years ago, I was attending a networking meeting. Our chapter leader had just received some awful news about a family member. She stood up to run the meeting with tears running down her cheeks and tried to pretend that everything was okay. Our meetings were usually positive with a lot of energy. In my mind, her tears ruined the meeting. I remember thinking *this does not belong here.*

At the time, I was majorly in the business of covering up my authentic self. I would have never wanted to let my networking group see that I was *weak*. Now I'm all about being who I really am, even if it means admitting my challenges. It is only out of being your authentic self that you can truly inspire others.

The Message

Speak your truth. What is it you REALLY should/need to say to your best client or your top referral partner? Do you always say what's on your heart? Here's the thing – when you don't speak your truth, you don't allow yourself to have the best relationships possible. Trust yourself. Trust in your relationship. Say what you have to say.

I can remember attending a workshop with entrepreneurs I had just met, some I had known for maybe a year, and a few for several years. In the process of doing some of this work, my passion for being the real me and helping others do the same, led me to share a huge chunk of my story. At the end, one of the men I had known for several years came up and hugged me. He looked me deep in the eyes and said, "Teri, you have always been awesome, but now, you are extraordinary."

I spent years not wanting the professionals I knew – especially the men – to know about who I really was and about my past. I wanted them to think I was perfect. I thought they wouldn't like me if they knew the embarrassing truth.

Instead of walking on eggshells worrying about what others will think of me, it's such an amazing gift to be loved for who you really are.

Fuel for your flame:
Am I being the real me?
Who can I begin being more real with today?

Chapter 45: Wonderment
by Sheli G

I adore this fun, interesting word. Wonderment is being in awe of, marveling at, pure joy, or a pleasant surprise.

For example, the wonderment of a great new idea or vision for a business, cause, or an invention, or the wonderment of a new relationship and all of the surprise, anticipation, and interesting things that we experience and learn along the way.

When we think of wonderment, we think of children playing or visions of going somewhere exotic for vacation, taking in new sights, smells, cultures, and the bliss of it all.

The Message
The truth is we're all just big kids, and we, too, love the sense of wonderment.
We love the feeling of adventure, having fun and laughing. Many of us don't do that enough.

We struggle to make time to have those experiences in our lives and in our businesses; times that will leave us feeling beyond blessed. *The feeling of anticipation, exhilaration, even euphoria needs to happen more!*

We can have that as entrepreneurs.
In fact, I would suggest you *should* have that. If you don't have it at least sometimes, maybe you're not really on the right path.

We need wonderment, excitement, anticipation, and joy, even amidst the challenges and struggles, which are always going to show up in life. It's part of the contract of being a human being: the highs and the lows, the ups, the downs, the challenges...but then the wonderment and the excitement, too.

If we ever lose that sense of excitement in our business or in our lives, that's where people can begin to feel lost.
That can lead us to not feeling fulfilled at our core, and we can only stay at that grind for so long, whether it's months or years, *before burnout is inevitable.*

Wonderment rules apply to us as adults.
Are we blocking out times to mastermind about new fun ways that we can approach our businesses, our goals, our teams? Finding interesting, fresh ways we can brainstorm and look at the new trends of marketing, what's exciting, and what is sexy and fun about what's going on in the world? What's trending? What's colorful? What's true? What's positive? What are people excited about? *What are people into right now, and what is lighting them up?*

We can look right now and ask, what excites our customers? What gets them fired up? Who's our target market? Where do they go play? Where do they go eat when they're hungry? Where do they hang out with their friends, and what do they talk about? How can we harness fun and intrigue in our businesses?

If we get bored with our vision, our teams and customers are going to be bored, too.
If we can't get re-inspired and re-fueled by our own vision, we're in trouble. Work is not the only thing that should fill up your soul. We talk about balance, and balance is kind of bogus or at least subjective. I don't know what balance looks like for you, *because it looks really individualized for each of us.*

Spending strategic time in the different areas of our lives, based on our values and priorities helps us all to be more balanced. Wonderment isn't just about the work. It's about finding harmony with your family. It's about finding joy and making sure you have good self-care so that you stay healthy, regenerated, and rejuvenated for all the things you're going to do. It's about protecting our children's sense of playful abandon and letting them have places where they can be free, wild, laugh, (be childlike!), *and not have to be appropriate or quiet.*

Great charities throw some of the most audacious parties.
They're so creative, over the top, grandiose, and people just love to go have fun at them. People will spend huge amounts of money to go, just to have a blast and revel in the excitement of it all. Charities have discovered people will donate money if they create a wonderment playground for adults.

In our businesses, our visions, and our teams, there's got to be enough enthusiasm to keep us engaged and excited month after month, year after year, and even decade after decade, or we're going to lose that fire inside of us.
Have a continuously kindled spirit, and be fully invested in what you're doing.

Wonderment can be hard to get back once you've lost it.
If you go too long in burnout mode, too long removed from your why, disconnected from any excitement, and without bliss and fulfillment in your business, it can be hard to find your way back to it.

So, it's important to never lose it. Never lose *why* you started down the road of what you're doing. What's exciting about that? What's positive about that? What is true about it? *What good is it doing?*

Maybe it's your product. Maybe it's your service. How are you serving the planet and making it a better world? *We all have the ability to create quality amazingness. How do we not lose our sense of wonderment?*

Through so many of these chapters, we've been talking about this theme of community, and that is not a coincidence.
Sustainable wonderment comes from the culture of the people in your teams and in your business. Make sure that you're surrounding yourself with people that really enjoy what they do and really want to do what they're doing. People who are not

just producing because they *have to*. They're not just producing to make a paycheck. That's a short-term model, and it certainly won't produce fulfillment.

But, people who are in the right roles, who are able to use their strengths, those who are able to feel that they make a tangible, significant difference, they will be excited.

Creating a positive culture doesn't mean a perfect culture.
Where there are humans, there are mistakes. We can learn and evolve. Continuing to be positive, supporting one another, listening to one another and creating safe places to do that, continuing to let people have a voice into things and inject new ideas, new enthusiasm, new blood, fresh approaches to things…*that's all really important in keeping wonderment.*

Another key is keeping extremely current on the times.
I see so many antiquated businesses with dusty philosophies and dated slogans. Even their logos are out of style. The way that they're doing management is out of touch or even extinct. Their office furniture, or office surroundings are old fashioned, tired, and dingy.

We need refreshers.
Whether it's remodeling the office, moving to a newer, brighter location, or to a better part of town, it might be time, because things change. Nothing is static. The culture is constantly moving. Technology is constantly updating. Sometimes you need a new website or you may need a total brand makeover.

Sometimes you need to update your company's colors, not just for the sake of change, but to be relevant and to keep things fresh, new, and inspiring. If you're not inspired by your logo any more, nobody else is going to be either. If you're not enthused by your philosophies and your value statements, maybe you need to go back to those and make sure those are still true and congruent for you in *this* moment. Maybe you need to do some focus groups and see if it's still creating a draw for your clientele, your target market, and demographic.

We must be open to change, or we will become obsolete.
Staying in a constant sense of wonderment means staying really relevant, and looking at not just how to keep up with the *right now*, but with *what's next*. What's next in my profession, my industry, my cause, my calling? What are people doing now, but where are people headed? Where are they focused? What are they wanting? What are they wanting that none of us are doing yet, and how can I help facilitate that in some way, small or big? How am I advertising? Is it fun? Is it fresh? Is it engaging? If I didn't know anything about this business, would I even look twice at my ad? Would I click on it? Would I pay what I'm asking people to pay?

Keeping the excitement going in your business has a lot to do with YOU as the leader, the center of the wheel.

You deserve to stay really engaged and passionate.
Sometimes you may just need to get away to go refuel yourself: body, mind, and spirit. You may need to go up to the mountains and just read books, hike, fish, watch movies, drink coffee...and just relax and remember how blessed you are! Take a timeout to remember why you began, and count how many amazing things have happened along the way. *Take time to acknowledge all the great lessons that have come from the challenges, and be grateful.*

A gratitude journal is a great way to document and journal how many highlights we have in our life.
It works well, because otherwise, we're always off to the next goal or task. We may have days with many successes, but we're off to the next thing, conquering our to-do list. Wait...take time to celebrate. Take time to revel in achievements.

Just the fact we can breathe, we're walking around, and have the minds to create amazing things is awesome!
The fact that we can be in relationship with so many different

people all over the world is incredible. I can Skype with people in Japan right now! What an awesome opportunity! *What a phenomenal time for invention and innovation at the highest levels.*

Consider sometimes taking that trip and unplugging, getting off your computer, getting off the phone, just unhooking from all that technology. Get out into the woods, the beach, the ski slopes, fields of flowers, or get into that hot tub and revel in the mystery and the magnitude of life itself.

What if everyone woke up in wonderment every day?
What if we woke up and asked, "How can I be positive today starting in my own home, and then spreading it out into my neighborhood?" Maybe I could rake some leaves or shovel snow anonymously. Maybe I could go to work and give somebody a hug or a smile; someone who I can tell really needs it. I could buy somebody a coffee – a gesture that says to them, *I was thinking about you.* Maybe I bring an amazing idea to the table. Maybe I support somebody else's incredible idea.

People that wake up in a space of gratitude, or they wake up and choose to get into a state of positivity — whether it's by meditating, praying, positive music, exercising — *they have already succeeded that day.*

What would our home be like?
You know, it's so easy with technology to be present, yet absent. Sometimes I'm as guilty as anyone else, like when my kids are on an iPad or a cell phone. They've grown up having games and movies at their fingertips. I started this thing that a friend of mine does with his kids. On the way to school, we unplug. We put those techy things away, and we talk about what we're grateful for. It's this amazing thing for me and my two kids, Teisha who's ten and Traden who's seven.

We talk about being grateful for the sun and the warmth that it gives us. We talk about being grateful we have a car that gets us to school and work. We talk about being grateful for our family. We talk about gratitude for our favorite foods. We talk about honoring God and the way He empowers us to serve others.

It's such a cool thing. It's easy, free, and it makes such a difference in the Wonderment mindset.
If we all did that as often as possible, intentionally, hour by hour, day by day, what kind of change could we cause? What kind of joy could come back, not only into our homes, but then transfer into our businesses, our causes, and our callings?

If we were those kind of Ignited Entrepreneurs, how could that not be contagious?!
When you're around somebody that's fired up, someone who comes up with great ideas, someone who's smiling, passionate, and who's willing to give a free hug, that's an awesome space to be in, isn't it? Who do you know like that?

When someone is honest, and even when it's not going well, they say, "Yeah, today's kind of challenging, but you know what? I'm going to hang in there." When you're around somebody who's constantly on the cutting edge of what is new, what's coming and how to be right in the middle of that, it's refreshing. When we see someone who's passionate about what they do because they're following the calling of their heart (not just what they've been told to do or what society says is a good job), the thing they know when they dip into their intuitive selves is the thing they're supposed to do, *that's inspiring to us all!*

As a coach, I know we all feel misunderstood on some level.
If you're doing something bold, if you're leading, and if you're thinking about the *what's next*, people are not always going to understand you.

My friend, Derrick Boles and I recently spoke about leadership. Leadership can feel lonely, and that sounds crazy to people, since leaders are typically surrounded by people! Great leaders have great influence; not just influencing themselves and what they do day to day, but they influence the people around them to be their highest and best selves.

How can an influencer be lonely when you're often surrounded by people?

If you've experienced it, you understand. It's an interesting sense of loneliness, because so many people *don't* live out the calling that is on their heart and mind. Too many people don't take those risks and step into courage. *In fact, it's rare to find the brave few who do.*

I believe the mantle of wonderment is on us as leaders and entrepreneurs, maybe more than on anyone else.

To whom much is given, much is indeed expected. You have been given great abilities. You know that or you wouldn't be reading this book! And, maybe even as you read this book, there are times you wonder about being the next Ignited Entrepreneur? Can I be the *what's next* in leadership? Am I going places? The answer is resoundingly yes, yes, yes!

I'm so passionate as I'm writing this to you right now, and I mean this with all my heart. These aren't just words to me. I wish I could convey it. You absolutely have everything inside of you already to be the most magnificent leader of our time. *You.* Not somebody else. If we all rise up, and if we all supported each other and quit competing, *we wouldn't have to walk on anybody else to achieve our wildest dreams.*

When I was taking that first intensive personal development class, *I had a long way to go to learn about true leadership and the totality of leadership.*

We were playing a game where there were four quadrants drawn with tape on this big floor. There were 30 of us on my team. We had to honestly judge ourselves and vote between four answers. On this three-month long personal development course, we had to honestly answer whether we were: 1. Playing to WIN,

2. Mostly Playing to Win, 3. Not playing to Win, or 4. Not playing at all.

Our staff of ten had to judge all of us, casting a vote as well. Then, we each had to judge each other. After all of those scores were totaled, we got in the boxes that we landed in based on all those scores. It was another one of those incredibly transformational moments of my life.

I ended up in that box of "Playing to WIN." I had judged myself as playing to win, because I really had. I had left it all on the floor, so-to-speak. I had done everything in my power at that time to learn, grow, be present, be real, honest, and available. And, my teammates also had judged me as playing to win, which was cool, and so did the staff.

But, as I looked around the room, I noticed that I was the *only* one in the 'playing to win' box.
As I looked next to me, there were a few people in the 'mostly playing to win' box, and then in the next box, there were a larger number of people in the 'sort of playing to win' category. Then, there were yet more people in the final box of 'not really playing.' It was disheartening. I was the only one in that 'playing to win' box. It wasn't like this epic moment where I was proud of myself. It was very interesting, and the facilitator then came to me and said something I will never forget. She said, "How does it feel to be in that box, AND be all alone?" She didn't say it judgmentally, she wasn't condemning me.

It was a huge *ah-ha* moment; a significant breakthrough. I realized I am in this box alone, and it doesn't feel good. She said, "A true leader not only plays to win, and you have, but the other part about the best and highest form of leadership, and which so many people miss, is that *a true leader brings a lot of other people with him to that winning box.*"

Wow! What a paramount truth. Are you ready? Find your sense

of Wonderment. Then keep it, kindle it, and share it. Help bring others to their state of passion and purpose. *You will never be the same once you realize the joy in doing that.*

The Ignited Entrepreneur **cannot help but ignite the best in others. Here's to your flame!**

Fuel for your flame:
Do you feel passion and wonderment in what you do? How can you keep that alive or rekindle it when it's running low?
How can you find that in your life if you don't have it now? Or, if you do, how can you assist others in finding theirs?

Sheli G and Terilee are inspirational to all business entrepreneurs. They have a "never quit" attitude you can experience in *The Ignited Entrepreneur*. They have modeled beautifully to me how women can keep going under any circumstance with grace.

Sue Macartney, Master Image Consultant, Owner of YOUR COLOR COSMETICS

Entrepreneurism is not a career choice, it's a calling. I believe it's a calling that everyone has with the right amount of insight and courage, which is exactly why you need to read this book!

Justin Foster, Brand strategist/author/speaker. **Fosterthinking.com**

Mind Map Example:

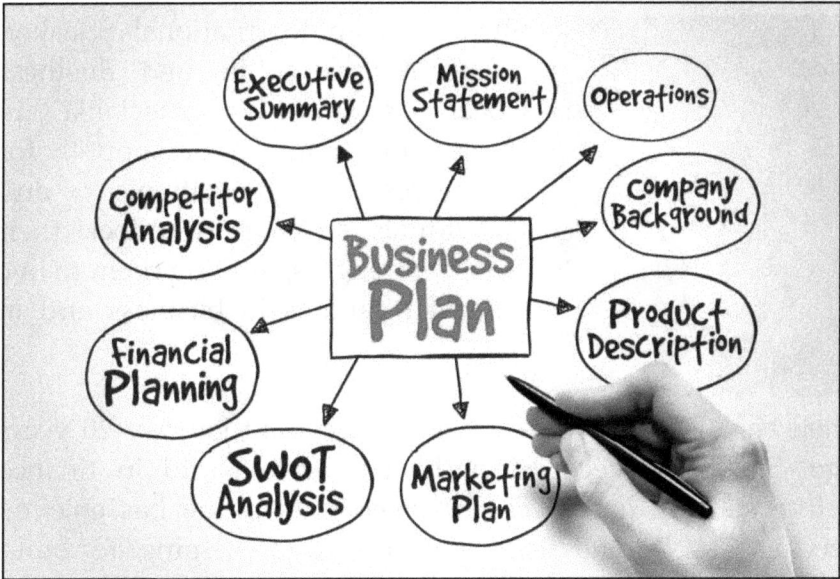

What's Next?

To schedule an "Ignited Entrepreneur Workshop" in your area or with your team with Terilee and Sheli G, contact us at **TerileeTalks@gmail.com**.

About Sheli G

Sheli G is an International Speaker, Master Certified Life and Business Coach, and is a specialist in Transformational Workshops for businesses, organizations, and individuals striving to unlock their highest strengths, igniting them to live out their callings in business and in life.

Sheli began her own personal development journey 20 years ago. She broke records in the corporate world in finance before starting her *serial entrepreneurialism*. She has enjoyed serving on various boards of directors, helping to build curriculum, hire facilitators, and re-align personal development tools for the current culture. Sheli has become certified herself as a Master Life Coach and Facilitator.

Since age 26, Sheli has been an entrepreneur, enjoying several businesses along the journey. Currently, she enjoys keynote speaking at conferences and events worldwide, as well as facilitating her Transformational Workshops and leading Life and Business hybrid mastermind groups and conferences. She also enjoys coaching CEO's, celebrities and executives to reach their next level UP. Sheli G makes her home in the gorgeous Treasure Valley of Idaho, with her husband Steve and their three miraculous children, Tyger, Teisha K, and Trae.

You can find her online at **www.SheliG.com** and on Facebook, LinkedIn, and Twitter. To hire Sheli G for your event or team, email her today at **sheliGcoaching@gmail.com**.

About Terilee Harrison

Terilee Harrison is a transformational leader, master teacher, author of *The Shameless Life*, and co-Author of *The Ignited Entrepreneur*. She is the CEO/Founder of Terilee Harrison International.

Since 2006, her life's work has been to educate, transform, and inspire people to live brilliant and bold lives of purpose.

An expert in business networking and relationship marketing, Terilee has worked with thousands of entrepreneurs at TEAM Referral Network in Southern California. She creates and leads transformational trainings that guide people to life and business mastery.

As a professional speaker, Terilee's ability to both inspire and challenge audiences to action and change can be attributed to her consistently authentic presentation regarding who she is, where she's been, and what she's learned along the way.

Terilee resides in Quartz Hill, California, with her husband, Terry. Together, they have four children.

You can find her online at **www.terileetalks.com**.

The Ignited Entrepreneur is proudly published by:

Creative Force Press
Guiding Aspiring Authors to Release Their Dream

www.CreativeForcePress.com

Do You Have a Book in You?

www.ingramcontent.com/pod-product-compliance
Lightning Source LLC
Chambersburg PA
CBHW052035090426
42739CB00010B/1918